44 ways to talk to your
ANGELS

44 ways to talk to your
ANGELS

connect with the angels' love and healing

JAYNE WALLACE AND LIZ DEAN

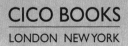

CICO BOOKS

LONDON NEW YORK

This edition published in 2019 by CICO Books
An imprint of Ryland Peters & Small Ltd

20–21 Jockey's Fields   341 E 116th St
London WC1R 4BW   New York, NY 10029
www.rylandpeters.com

10 9 8 7 6 5 4 3 2

Text © Jayne Wallace and Liz Dean 2014
Design and illustration © CICO Books 2014

First published in 2014

Neither the authors nor the publishers can be held responsible for any claim arising out of the use or misuse of suggestions made in this book. The suggestions in this book are not intended to replace diagnosis of illness or ailments, or healing or medicine. Always consult your doctor or other health professional in the case of illness. Essential oils are very powerful and potentially toxic if used too liberally. Please follow the advice given on the label and never use the oils neat on bare skin, or if pregnant.

A CIP catalog record for this book is available from the Library of Congress and the British Library.

ISBN: 978 1 78249 704 2

Printed in China

Editor: Rosie Lewis
Designer: Gail Jones
Illustrator: Sarah Perkins

Contents

Introduction

How did this book come to you?

If you're reading this, your angels have a message for you. Maybe you have sensed their guidance in unexpected ways—repeating numbers, unusual dreams, a tingling on your skin, a little feather in an unexpected place. All these and more are heaven-sent signs from your angels, who come to guide and protect you as you take the next steps along your life path.

We all have a life path, a blueprint that is with us the moment we are born. This life path offers us experiences we need to have so that our soul can evolve. Our angels help us follow our destiny in this lifetime. Their gifts are many and infinite, and include support, unconditional love, non-judgment, healing, compassion, direction, self-trust, and spiritual development. Your relationship with your angels helps you see your true self—not the "ego" self, but who you are as a spiritual, loving being at the level of your soul.

Angels will always help you. You can call upon your angels for little things and for help with bigger challenges, from finding a parking space to seeing a way forward in your work, and from attracting a new relationship to healing the past and discovering your life purpose. Angels love you unconditionally and do not judge you. If you ask and trust, they will come. This book will show you how.

Jayne and I wrote this book because we felt the call of our angels. We trusted the guidance we were given, and began work long before we showed it to our publisher and illustrator, Sarah Perkins, who thankfully shared our vision.

We are deeply grateful for the opportunity to share our lifetime experiences with you in these 44 magical ways.

Liz Dean and Jayne Wallace

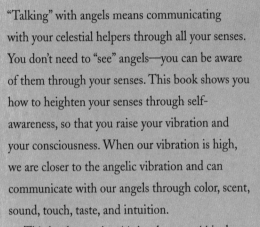

How to Use this Book

This book offers you techniques for meeting your angels, allowing your relationship to grow so that you develop spiritually and feel their amazing love and guidance in every aspect of your life.

"Talking" with angels means communicating with your celestial helpers through all your senses. You don't need to "see" angels—you can be aware of them through your senses. This book shows you how to heighten your senses through self-awareness, so that you raise your vibration and your consciousness. When our vibration is high, we are closer to the angelic vibration and can communicate with our angels through color, scent, sound, touch, taste, and intuition.

This book contains 44 tips, because 44 is the number of the angels (for more on angel numbers, see Tip 2). To choose a tip, go to whichever page you feel drawn to first. It may be the color of the illustration that attracts you, or a word that catches your eye. Go with your first impression.

You can also make a ritual of choosing a tip. Close your eyes, and flick through the pages from the front of the book to the back (or back to front, if you're left-handed). As you do this, ask your angels to stop you when you have reached the tip you need today.

In some tips, we give you meditations that call upon particular angels or archangels. You don't need to call upon the angel we recommend—you can call upon your guardian angel (see page 13) or simply say "My Angels", the angels who can help you most will always join you. At the back of the book is an Angel Directory, which lists 44 archangels and angels. These angels help with different life areas. You can call upon any of these angels, too, if you feel they suit your intention.

Finally, you will find channeled messages from your angels on page 141. You can meditate on these, or write them out to make message cards (see Tip 39).

Throughout, we've referred to angels as "he," but when you connect with your angels, you may feel that their presence is feminine, masculine, or neither. Whatever you sense is perfect and right for you.

Before You Begin

Most of the rituals and meditations ask you to ground, protect, and open up before you begin—grounding is to keep yourself centered and connected to the earth, while "opening up" means opening a channel of communication with your angels through being in a "feeling" place, rather than using your thoughts.

When you have finished your meditation or ritual, you should always close down—shutting the communication door to the angelic realms and coming back into the here and now.

With practice, you will be able to ground, protect, open up, and close down quickly, and it will soon feel like second nature.

Grounding and Protection

Staying grounded during a meditation helps you maintain a connection with the earth when you are traveling to other levels of awareness and communicating with the angelic realms. You need to ground yourself first by visualizing roots growing from the soles of your feet into the earth, going deeper and deeper. Here's how:

* Sit comfortably. Take some relaxing deep breaths and focus on the soles of your feet, feeling them planted firmly on the floor. Feel the weight of your body in your feet. Now imagine that roots are growing from the soles of your feet deep into the earth. As you do this, you can visualize the colors of the earth—brown and deep red—as your roots go deeper and deeper.

* Now anchor your roots. Imagine great boulders of crystal near the earth's core. See your roots twining around these crystal boulders (you can visualize your favorite crystal for this, if you like). You are rooted in the earth, supported and safe.

After grounding, you need to protect yourself from negative or distracting energies from other people:

* Imagine that you are in a protective bubble. It is wide and high enough for you to reach around in every direction, and it is transparent, so that you can still see and feel everything. Imagine that your bubble is a force field, repelling any negative energy.

* Now imagine sealing your bubble so that nothing can enter. You can see this as like tying the top of a balloon, or imagine that you have a big zipper in the front of your bubble—zip it right

up to the top. When you have done this, you might like to visualize a symbol at the top of your bubble, such as a gold or silver star. You might see this naturally.

Opening Up: The Breathing-Connection Technique

Now you are ready to open up, to open your awareness so that you can attune to the angelic vibration. We do this through the breath, and using visualization:

* Lie down or sit comfortably.
* Turn your attention to your breathing. Breathe slowly and deeply, and become aware of the energies around you. Tune in to your senses and really feel your breath flowing in and out of your body. If you like, you can try breathing in for a count of five, then out for five. Take shallower breaths when you feel ready.
* Visualize energy coming up from your roots, then through your feet, up through your legs, through the base of your spine/genital area, up through your sacral chakra (below your navel), and into your solar plexus. Move the energy up into your heart, your throat, your third eye (between your brows), and up to the crown of your head. See the energy flowing from the crown of your head up to the angelic realms and your angels.

* Sense your angels sending energy back down through your whole body—through the crown of your head, through your third eye, throat, heart, and solar plexus, then down through your sacral and base chakras, through your feet, and back down to the earth again. Feel this energy flowing through you. It is the pure white light of your angels.
* Now imagine a small wheel at your solar plexus. This will be the "exchange point" for your energy with the angels' energy so that they can fill you with light.
* See the wheel turning, bringing up energy from the earth through your feet to your solar plexus. As the wheel turns, it is also bringing down pure, white angelic light from the angelic realms to your solar plexus. Here the energy is exchanged—the angels are pouring light into your body and you are sending up your energy for them to purify from your feet, through your legs, base of spine, navel area, up to the solar plexus.
* You might see the energy coming up from your feet as darker energy at first, then becoming lighter as you breathe. As you keep breathing, keep this exchange going by focusing on your solar plexus, and feel your whole body expanding and filling with light.

✳ Sense this lovely angelic light vibration. You might feel a wave of relaxation as your angels' vibrations uplift you.

When you're moving energy in this way, it flows freely through the seven major chakra points on your body. You might see your chakras as colors and sense their different vibrations, or visualize them as spinning wheels of energy; others see them as small doors that open up, or as vibrantly colored flowers. When the chakras open, you might experience this as spinning energy vortexes or flowers that transform from buds to full bloom. But it's fine if you sense something different. Whatever you experience is perfect.

Closing Down

When you have finished your meditation, you must close down every time by closing your chakras. This is to protect you from being exposed to other people's energies—the vibration of their thoughts, feelings, and sensations. You can do this by visualizing the chakras closing in this order: crown, third eye, throat, heart, solar plexus, sacral, then base. If you see your chakras as doors, close them down by seeing each little door close in turn. If you see your chakras as flowers, close them down by closing the petals of each flower. You might see one type of flower, such as a rose, with a different color for each chakra; or you might see a different flower for each chakra, such as:

Our developing chakras

Since about 15,000 BCE, chakras have been identified as spinning vortexes of energy located in the human energy field. There are seven principal chakras and hundreds of minor chakra points. Each chakra has particular qualities, and the balanced or imbalanced energy of each one tells a healer about the emotional, mental, physical, and spiritual health of a person. As we raise our consciousness through self-awareness and communication with our angels, guides, and other beings in the spiritual realms, "new" chakras are awakened, known as the developing, or multidimensional chakras (see Tip 36).

- **Crown:** white lily
- **Third eye:** purple freesia
- **Throat:** blue cornflower
- **Heart:** pink rose or green chrysanthemum
- **Solar plexus:** sunflower or buttercup
- **Sacral:** orange gerbera
- **Base:** red poppy

It can be helpful to use a slow count of three for closing each chakra. When all your chakras are fully closed, your protective bubble can disappear, and you can open your eyes and gently readjust to your surroundings.

The more you practice this, the faster you will become, and you'll be able to open up and close down quite quickly whenever you have a moment or two to tune into your angels. In a nutshell:

- Ground
- Protect
- Open up
- Close down

The Seven Principal Chakras

7. Crown

6 Third eye

5 Throat

4 Heart

3 Solar Plexus

2 Sacral

1 Base

The Developing Chakras

Stellar gateway

Soul star

Fourth eye

Angelic

Higher heart

Heart seed

Hara

Earth star

(see also Tip 36)

The Chakras and Their Colors

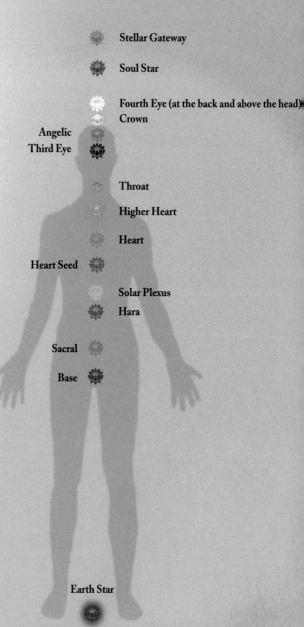

Stellar Gateway

Soul Star

Fourth Eye (at the back and above the head)
Crown

Angelic
Third Eye

Throat

Higher Heart

Heart

Heart Seed

Solar Plexus

Hara

Sacral

Base

Earth Star

Three Ways to Meet Your Guardian Angel

We are all born with a guardian angel, whether we know it or not. In the precious hours before your birth, your guardian angel appears, watching you come safely into the world. Whatever happens throughout your life, your guardian angel never leaves you, and will always try to protect you and keep you on your life path. You may meet other angels along the way, who help and guide you—just like friends you meet who may stay with you for months, years, or most of a lifetime—but your guardian angel is with you always.

To meet your guardian angel, you can explore any of the three meditations shown on the following pages. You might like to try 1 to begin with, or try 2 and 3 in succession—you can blend 2 and 3 together by asking your guardian angel to take you to the crystal cave after you've flown around the galaxy!

Why Meditation?

Meditation and ritual create a pathway to the angelic realms. They allow your "feeling" energy to make a link, as if growing a fiber-optic cable between you. When you are connected with your angels, you can communicate through all your senses, and receive love, healing, protection, and more. A meditation is time spent with your angels, and it can last a minute or an hour; as time has no meaning for angels, one minute might feel like an hour, or vice versa. However long you spend with your angels, one of these rituals and meditations will be perfect for you.

Your guardian angel may give you their name. This may be a name you have heard before—one of the archangels, such as Michael, Gabriel, or Raphael. If you don't receive a name, you can give your guardian angel a name based on how they look or feel, a descriptive name such as Blue Angel or White Angel, or simply call them My Angel or

Guardian Angel. Many people don't get a name for their guardian angel, but if you do, it's usually the first name that you sense or hear when you connect. You can ask for confirmation of this name over the next few weeks—for example, if you sense that your guardian angel's name is Joseph, you might see this name in a prominent way in your everyday life—it could be a new person you meet, or a name on a billboard or letter. But don't strive to find a name. It's fine for your guardian angel just to be your guardian angel.

If you are given the name of your angel, quietly address them. And whenever you ask your angel for help, begin by calling their name: "Angel Joseph, please help me …"

Your guardian angel will always offer you love, protection, and healing, but you can also call on other angels you feel drawn to (see Meet Your Guardian Angel, Tip 3). Your guardian angel won't be offended—in fact, he or she will help you connect with other helper angels. You might also like to call upon Archangel Barachiel, the chief of the guardian angels, to help you connect with your guardian angel for the first time. Another angel who can help you meet your guardian angel is Archangel Metatron, who is known as the guardian of all guardian angels (see the Angel Directory, page 136.)

Preparing To Meet Your Guardian Angel

To meet your angel, all you have to do is be open and ready to receive. This means emptying your mind and letting go of distractions. Just like decluttering your home, you'll need to declutter your thoughts to make space for your angels to "come home" to you and find a connection with them through your heart. Try not to judge yourself or have expectations; be open to whatever you receive.

Read through the three meditations first, then choose one that appeals. You might find it helpful to record yourself reading the meditation first, then play it back when you are ready to try it. You can play gentle music to set the scene, too, as it creates a soothing vibration.

MEET YOUR GUARDIAN ANGEL 1:
THE MAGIC GARDEN

* Sit or lie down comfortably and close your eyes. If you have a favorite stone or crystal, hold it in the palm of your hand. Now ground and protect yourself (see pages 9–10)—feel roots growing from the soles of your feet deep into the earth, then see yourself in a bubble that encloses the whole of your body.
* Follow this process with your breath (see page 10). Focus on your breathing, and on the feeling of angelic light filling your body. If your thoughts and worries begin to intervene, become

a witness—step back and see them drift away in front of you. Breathe them out.

* Really feel the angelic light in your whole body. Now ask your guardian angel to come close to you. See yourself in your mind's eye, being ready to meet someone.

* Visualize yourself sitting on a bench in a garden. This is a magical garden, full of flowers. You might smell grass or the fragrance of a particular bloom, or sense sunshine on your arms or face. You are feeling deeply relaxed and safe.

* Pay attention to everything you feel and "see"— a tingling sensation on a particular part of your body, such as your cheek, or along one arm, or your hair being touched. You may actually perceive an angelic form. You might see flowers of different colors. There might be the sensation of deep calm and love. Some people feel tearful in angelic presence without "seeing" an angel's form or angel wings; they just know that angels are with them. Others get an initial, a color, a whisper.

Did your angel show you a color or give you a name? Quietly address them by speaking their name; this strengthens your connection.

* When you sense the energy of your guardian angel pull back, thank them and see yourself sitting on your garden bench again, alone. Hold the feeling you had of your angel's presence. What was it like?

* Switch your focus back to your gentle breathing, and open your eyes. You have now connected with your guardian angel.

* Close down (see page 11).

Did You Meet Someone Else?

Did you meet someone else on the bench? You might have sensed someone you knew who is now in spirit, or met your spirit guide for the first time. Like your guardian angel, your spirit guide is there to help keep you on your life path. Spirit guides have lived as humans on earth, whereas angels generally have never been human and exist only in the heavenly realms. Many people are aware that they have both spirit guides and angels around them.

If you didn't meet angels or guides this time, all you need to do is keep practicing this meditation and become used to being open and relaxed; the more comfortable you are with yourself, and the more focused and calm, the more likely you are to be receptive to your angels. Trust that as long as you remain open to them, they will be with you, and when you are ready, they will communicate.

Angels can make themselves known to you whether you meditate to meet them or not. As you will see in this book, you can sense your angel's presence through signs they leave for us, through other earthly people, music, scent, crystals, and more.

MEET YOUR GUARDIAN ANGEL 2:
THE COSMIC WISDOM JOURNEY

* Sit or lie down comfortably and close your eyes. If you have a favorite stone or crystal, hold it in the palm of your hand or place it on your heart chakra. Now do the grounding exercise only (see pages 9–10). We use the protective bubble as part of this meditation.

* Begin to pay attention to your breathing. Take some slow, deep breaths, then visualize white light coming toward you. Breathe the light deeply into your abdomen and feel it expand. Let it move up into your heart and see the light expanding there. Do this three or four times, exhaling anything other than light—tiredness, negativity, old thoughts. See the light illuminating your throat and head, right up to your crown. You're feeling light, as though you might float off the floor or chair.

* Now see the light inside you radiate, making a bubble of light that encloses you. You're completely in this bubble, and you can see out perfectly; you are drifting in your bubble into a white room. Imagine the feeling of peace in this pure space. Call upon your guardian angel, asking him to join you, saying: "My guardian angel, please come and stand behind me."

* Now feel the power of your angel very close to you. You might feel a tingling around your shoulders as your angel envelops you with his wings and gently lifts you higher. You are completely safe and loved. Your angel will now reach for your hand and take you flying. Trust your angel to guide you as you float together over the clouds, up to the heavens, and into the galaxy. There are stars everywhere.

* Now you can ask your guardian angel questions. Do you want to know his or her name? Or, you might ask who you are in the universe and what you need to do in this lifetime. What do your dreams mean? You may just ask your guardian angel about healing or helping you find wisdom. You could also ask about a person and their well-being.

* When you are ready, your angel will return you to the white room—you are still in your light bubble. Thank your angel as you sense them stepping back. Let yourself and your bubble land, and see yourself lying or sitting down, stretching out into your physical body. Begin to feel the weight of your body on the floor or chair. You might start to move your body slightly.

* Close down (see page 11).

MEET YOUR GUARDIAN ANGEL 3:

THE CRYSTAL CAVE

* Follow the meditation as for 2 and lay down with a favorite crystal. This time place it on your heart chakra. Ground yourself (see pages 9–10), then open up by breathing in white light. Put yourself in a bubble of white light, and go to the white room. As before, call upon your guardian angel, asking him to stand behind you.
* Feel the power and protection as your angel envelops you with his wings and gently lifts you up. See a door open in the white room.
* Your guardian angel floats you through this door. Inside is a crystal cave and before you is a bed made of sparkling crystals. There is light everywhere, glistening from the natural crystals that cover the cave. Lie down on the crystal bed and feel it vibrate with pure energy. Feel the crystal in your hand, and merge with its energy. Become one with the crystal. Melt into the crystal bed. Your guardian angel is standing by you. Absorb all the sensations and vibrations— really feel the energy and colors coming to you in this beautiful place.
* Now you can ask your guardian angel questions, and talk or listen.
* Other angels may visit. You may find yourself calling upon angels of healing, or angels of peace. You don't need to name them—it is enough just to say: "Healing angels, please come

closer." Thank your guardian angel and these other angels.
* Your guardian angel will know when to take you back to the white room. You will remember the colors from your experience in the cave, and other messages. Don't be concerned that you'll forget. Let your guardian angel take care of this for you.
* See yourself lying or sitting back down in your body as your guardian angel helps you and steps back. Feel his energy ebb, and begin to feel heavier in your body as you come back to the floor or chair.

What Colors Did You See?

The colors you see can relate to areas to work on. If you saw lots of pink in the crystal cave, for example, your focus is on love and relationships. First read Tip 8 about colors and angel meanings, then try the specific meditation for your color, as listed below:

Red: Security and change, *Tip 9*
Orange: Sexuality and self-expression, *Tip 10*
Yellow: Strength, energy and joy, *Tip 11*
Green: Healing, *Tip 12*
Pink: Love and relationships:, *Tip 13*
Blue: Speaking your truth, *Tip 14*
Purple: Insight and intuition, *Tip 15*
White: Spiritual development, *Tip 16*

part one:

The 44 Ways

1 Trusting the Signs of an Angel

Angels want to talk to you in your everyday world to help and guide you along your true path, and they often do this through angelic signs and symbols.

When you see a feather on the pavement on its own, rather than in a park, or perhaps a tiny butterfly winging its way past your tenth-floor office window, or a cloud formation that seems meaningful (see Tip 41), your angels are connecting with you. You might get a tingling sensation on one side, sometimes just on the scalp or hand, or over your whole body. Those who are guided by angels describe this as a buildup of excitement, the feeling that something intense is about to happen. You may feel a strong certainty about a decision you need to make, or the urge to make a call to someone for no logical reason. These experiences, and many more like them, mean that your angels are guiding you to follow your feelings, rather than what you think you should be doing. Decisions you make according to your heart will take you on the next step of your journey. As messengers of Spirit, God, the Source, the universe, the "All That Is"— angels connect you with your soul purpose.

Winged creatures are often a sign of spirit and your angels drawing closer to you. Not every bird or butterfly is an angelic sign; only the ones you really notice. Your noticing means that you are attuning to angelic energies, and once you notice one angel sign, it feels easy and natural to notice more. However, if you think too much about seeing angels and consciously look for signs, you may temporarily lose your link with your angels because your thoughts are overtaking your feelings and senses. Trust that when angels are ready to communicate with you, you will naturally notice their signs without having to try too hard. You don't need to take responsibility; your angels will get their message through.

THE SIGNS OF ANGELS

* Sensation: Tingling on your skin, or the sensation of cobwebs in your hair
* Thought communication: People around you saying the word "angel/s," or seeing it on social media
* Noticing the word "angel" in book titles and other media
* Seeing feathers where you wouldn't expect them
* Repeating numbers or number patterns, and the number 44 (see Tip 2)
* Seeing "flash" images that don't feel part of you (see How Do You See an Angel?, Tip 3)
* Finding pennies in the street

* A high-pitched buzzing in your ears before you go
to bed or when you wake up in the morning. This
is also associated with a rise in consciousness. If
you find it too loud, ask your guardian angel (see
page 13) to turn down the volume!

* Getting messages from Earth Angels (see
Tip 23).

As you practice working with your angels, you will
get to know their signs as ways to communicate
with you.

2 Angels are Close When You Notice Numbers

Did you wake up one night and look at your phone, or the clock and see 11, 22, 33, or 44? Are you seeing these numbers in other places too? If so, your angels are talking to you. Numbers are the codes of the angels.

When angels are trying to contact you, they give a number pattern—your lucky number not just once but three times in one day, for instance, perhaps in a phone number, barcode, or ticket, on an airline departures board, or as a significant date.

In numerology (the study of sacred numbers), all numbers have a vibration and a meaning. A proliferation of threes, and 33, means you are being told that soon there will be action and decisions, particularly relating to conception and creative projects. Three is the number of the Archangel Gabriel, messenger of God and the divine will (see Tip 44, page 126). The number 333 means The Ascended Masters—spiritual beings who are guiding you strongly from now on. The numbers 11 and 22 are spiritual power numbers: 11 signifies intuition and 22, manifests dreams into being. Numbers in sequence, such as 1, 2, 3, 4, or 5, 6, 7, can mean "stay focused— you're going in the right direction." However, the key message when you start noticing number patterns is just this—that you are noticing, and when this happens your angels are saying "I have a message for you." They have given you the special code, and now have your attention. Stop and breathe slowly, feeling the sensations around you. You might sense a whisper in your ear, or a word or image might suddenly come to mind. Even without specific signs such as these, noticing numbers and patterns means that you have support, are on the right path, and will be helped that day.

Forty-four is the number of the angels. When you see this number, the angels are showing you that you are strongly connected with them; they are letting you know that they are around you and ready to give you guidance. The message is "Be true to yourself. We will help you follow your path."

Four is a sacred number in Pythagorean philosophy. It stands for the four elements—Air, Earth, Water, and Fire—and the four directions, together representing the essence of the world. Four was believed to stand for wholeness, justice, and completion, and when added to 1, 2, and 3, gives 10, the number of the cosmos.

3 How Do You "See" an Angel?

Ask yourself: are you a highly visual person—perhaps you react strongly to color, clothes, interior design, and film? Is this your strongest sense? Or perhaps you're a "word" person—you're a reader or listener, and everything's about conversation; after you've finished watching a film it goes right out of your head. For this reason, you may also find it harder to visualize and meditate.

If you're strongly visual, you may be clairvoyant ("clear-seeing"). If words and sound are "you," you're dominantly clairaudient ("clear-hearing"). Your angels may talk to you via your dominant sense at first, because it's easiest for you at the beginning of your relationship. So for you, "seeing" an angel may mean hearing a whisper, sensing your angel's colors, or seeing angel signs (see Tip 1). As you attune to your angels, your vibration will lift so that you become more sensitive to their presence through your other senses, too—you'll start to be more aware of aromas, touch, even taste. "Seeing" your angels might mean feeling held, feeling calm and relaxed, smelling summer roses, or perhaps noticing a sweet taste in your mouth. All these experiences are equal. As you attune more to the angelic realms, you'll become familiar with how your angels let you know they are with you.

If you do angel card or tarot readings, you'll already have a strong idea of how messages tend to come through to you. For the medium Jackie Cox,

clairaudience is her dominant channel. "It feels as if they [angels and guides] are putting words into the front of my forehead, then saying the words to me. I hear the words. I rarely get pictures, showing me what's happened in a client's life. I just don't see that. Because I hear words, sometimes I go back to my angels and guides to check that I've heard the words correctly. I ask three times, 'Have I got this right?' They always let me know if I'm correct by giving me confirmation, usually goose bumps on my thighs! Then they push me to give the client those exact words, repeating them to me one more time. My clients often say, 'That is exactly what I was thinking,' or 'My mother used that exact phrase.'"

For Jayne, giving readings and picking up intuitive messages is like being in a never-ending movie. "I see a client's past, present, and future as a series of film clips," she says. "It's always in color, there's a full cast of characters—they [her angels and guides] just show me everything, and it's very fast. It's like I'm in two places at once—watching the movie of their life and telling them what I see as the film plays out."

The philosopher and esotericist Rudolf Steiner (1861–1925) explained how we might "see" angels and their hopes for future humanity as images, in a lecture he gave in Munich in October 1918, entitled "The Work of the Angels in Man's Astral Body" (the astral body is the fourth level of the aura, connected to the heart chakra):

"The Angels form pictures in man's astral body and these pictures are accessible to thinking that has become clairvoyant. If we are able to scrutinize these pictures, it becomes evident that they are woven in accordance with quite definite impulses and principles. Forces for the future evolution of mankind are contained in them. If we watch the Angels carrying out this work of theirs—strange as it sounds, one has to express it in this way—it is clear that they have a very definite plan for the future configuration of social life on earth; their aim is to engender in the astral bodies of men such pictures as will bring about definite conditions in the social life of the future."

SENSING YOUR ANGELS IN THE DARK

You will need a room with a mirror that you can sit in front of. A dresser with a mirror is ideal.

* Take a candle (this can be any candle you have to hand, of any color) and place it close to the mirror. Light the candle, turn off the lights in the room, and close the door. Ground, protect, and open up (see pages 9–10). Begin to feel your angels' vibrations as they join you in the room. You can ask your guardian angel to join you too, calling them by name.

* Close your eyes and visualize your angels, and begin to become sensitive to their presence, paying attention to all your senses. When you feel something, such as a change in temperature or a tingling sensation, your angels are with you. Now say to yourself, "I wish to see and commune with my angels."

* Half-open your eyes and gaze into the mirror. Allow your senses to open, embracing the energy of your angels. Trust what you are sensing.

* Accept all the sensations you receive. Don't try to "see" an angel; when you consciously will this to happen, your thinking mind jumps in and you are less present to messages or impressions you're being given. Relax, breathe, and focus on your feelings and senses to keep the connection between you and your angels strong.

WHAT DID YOU SENSE?

Trust yourself and your experience. Go with what happens naturally, because what happens naturally and quickly is right. You may sense a change in

color, or feel something in your peripheral vision; sometimes it may feel as though an image appears in your mind as if someone outside of you has just given you a picture. Describe the picture to yourself or out loud before you think about what it is or what it means. When you are finished, close down (see page 11).

ANGEL SCRYING IN A TEACUP OR BOWL

Scrying means seeing images in objects, traditionally stones with polished surfaces, such as a hematite mirror or crystal ball, which people meditated on to connect with other beings—angels and spirit guides—and to receive otherworldly signs and symbols. For this ritual, we make it easy and scry with water. You'll need a candle of any type, and a teacup, mug, or a bowl. Don't use your best china, as you'll be adding wax to the water. The best cups or bowls to use are dark on the inside.

* Fill your cup or bowl with water from the faucet. Call in your angels (remembering to ground, protect, and open up—see pages 9–10), and gaze into the water. Sense the vibration of your angels around you.
* Light the candle and let it burn for a minute or two to give enough wax to drip into the water. Now swirl the water around with a spoon, then remove the spoon and pour some wax into the swirling water, into the center of the cup or bowl.

* Look at the patterns the solidifying wax is making in the water. Trust what you see.
* Remember to close down when you are finished (see page 11), and thank your angels.

CLOUDS AND WINGS IN YOUR COFFEE CUP

When you drink a cappuccino, leave a little residue in the bottom of the cup. Better still, make a Greek or Turkish coffee and drink two-thirds of it, leaving lots of thick coffee grounds in the bottom of the cup. Now place the saucer on top of the cup with the handle toward you, turn both cup and saucer upside down, and leave for five minutes. Then turn the cup upright, put the saucer to one side, and look at the shape the cappuccino foam or coffee grounds have made on the inside of the cup. Do you see cloud shapes or wings? Coffee-cup reader Hulya Mehmet says:

* An angel wing or wings in your cup means your angels are protecting and guiding you
* Clouds: Light clouds are a message from the angels to follow your dream; darker clouds can show problems you will overcome
* The number 44 means the angels are with you.

4 How to Ask an Angel for Help, in Any Situation

One of the secrets of manifesting with angels is saying "Thank You" in advance of the wish being granted, trusting they will intervene to help you.

Aside from the courtesy of this, thanking your angels in advance of their assistance shows that you have complete faith that they can deliver what you are asking for. This is how manifesting works; your faith takes away any feelings of desperation or neediness that can get in the way of receiving. When you are needy, your vibration is lower than when you are feeling confident, calm, and believing. When you trust, you are not only trusting your angels to deliver, but also trusting yourself and the universe to meet your needs, guide you, and keep you safe. If you think you have problems with trust, consider how easy—or not—it is for you to ask for help from others. Do you have to be the one being the helper, and do you find it easier to give than to receive?

Not being able to accept support from others can indicate a lack of self-belief, seeing everyone else as more deserving. If you often feel small, ask your angels to empower you before you ask for your main wish. When you feel empowered, it's easier to trust; and when you trust yourself and your angels to do the right thing, your manifesting will be all the more effective. You can make your own dreams come true—with a little angelic help.

HOW TO ASK

* Ground and protect yourself, and open up (see pages 9–10). Really tune in to your angels' vibrations as they join you.

* Begin to set up a feeling of trust. If you find this difficult, begin by saying: "My Angels, please help me trust myself and you; give me the confidence to make my wish." Let the vibration of this request sit with you for a minute or two. Now push the vibration outward into your energy field. Feel the vibration expanding and growing stronger, and sense that you are feeling bigger.

* Ask your angels to grant whatever wish you have with genuine good feeling. What would it be like to have your wish granted? See yourself experiencing this, feeling happy, relieved, inspired.

* Now say "Thank you for making my wish come true." Your wish is with the angels and the universe, so step back and even try to forget about it for a time. Let your angels do their work. This way of asking your angels works for whatever request you have, wherever you are.

Whenever you ask your angels for help, remember: Feel it (emotions), sense it (using your senses), ask, say "thank you," and let go.

Provided your intentions are true, and your wish will not harm any other person or creature, your angels will help. You don't have to need something big or be in a crisis to ask your angels for guidance. Ask your angels when sitting by your angel altar; ask for a parking space when you're driving (see Tip 29); ask when you're at your desk or on your feet at work; ask when you're walking alone. Just ask.

5 Love Yourself First

Angels want you to love yourself first and foremost. It can feel easier to give other people the responsibility for loving you in return for helping them. Seeing yourself as a martyr to others' needs can also be a way of avoiding dealing with low self-esteem: if you stop "doing," who will love you?

Your angels can help you just be, not do. They love you unconditionally, but you need to love yourself first and, with your angels' support, heal any problems so that you can grow emotionally and spiritually. Shame and guilt are the two emotions that can be hardest to overcome, because by their very nature they want to remain hidden. This visualization can help because you focus on forgiveness. If you can forgive yourself for your past actions and forgive those who have hurt you, you remove the blocks to loving yourself and others. Negative emotions get trapped in your aura, and feeding them habitually with doses of resentment, hurt, and regret can take up a lot of your energy. When you release this negativity with forgiveness, you raise your vibrations, feel more loving and energized, and become happier with yourself as you are. Angel Raguel is the angel of forgiveness, so you might like to call him into this healing ritual.

Forgiveness Healing Ritual

Take a piece of paper. Write down things you want to forgive yourself for. Sometimes you might just feel uncomfortable about the past without knowing why. Try to describe these feelings in a few words. Now write down the names of one or two people you are angry at.

* Forgiveness is easy. Telling yourself this is the first step. Just ask your angels to join you, closing your eyes and breathing softly in and out (remember to do the grounding, protecting, and opening-up technique on pages 9–10 first). Follow the sound of your breathing as you sit comfortably, sensing your angels' loving vibrations. Call your angels by name, saying three times, "My Angels/Angel Raguel, please help me forgive myself and others, and love myself more. Guide and protect me. Thank you." Speak slowly, feeling your angels' wings around you, visualizing the words fading on the paper.

* Now take a crystal. You can use your dedicated angel crystal (see Tip 6), or merlinite or rhodonite, which are both stones of forgiveness.

Wrap the paper around the stone and tie it with ribbon or string or whatever you can find. Place the stone on your altar by an angel figurine, which will protect the ritual. Leave it here for 28 days, a lunar cycle, then take the paper from the stone and safely burn it in a candle flame or fire. This symbolically cleanses you of the past and signifies the end of the ritual.

You might also like to try the quick forgiveness fix in Tip 12.

6 Connecting with Angels through Crystals

Crystals are amazing transmitters of energy. There are hundreds of thousands of types of crystal of differing shapes and crystalline structures, and each has its own properties and type of vibration.

Crystals affect us on a physical, mental, emotional, and spiritual level, helping our internal energies align to bring about self-healing and give insight as to our states of being. Some crystals in particular help you connect with the angelic realms, but if you don't have any of those listed opposite or on page 34, you can use a clear quartz crystal, or any other crystal with which you have an affinity.

HOW TO BEGIN TO WORK WITH A CRYSTAL

First, cleanse your crystal by holding it under running water for a few moments. Alternatively, leave it in a bowl of salt overnight (ordinary table salt will do), or for at least an hour, making sure the crystal is completely immersed in the salt. You can also cleanse a crystal by leaving it to bathe in sunlight or moonlight. A fast way to cleanse crystals is by holding them in incense smoke or breathing on them. You can do this as follows:

* Hold your crystal gently. Breathe deeply and follow the sound of your breath. Imagine you are inhaling light, and gently exhale this light by blowing over your crystal to cleanse it. Do this for three or four deep breaths.

ATTUNING YOUR CRYSTAL TO YOUR ANGELS

* Before you begin, ground, protect, and open up to your angels (see pages 9–10). Visualize your angels or an archangel you would like to link your crystal with. See the particular angel/s in your mind's eye; you might see lots of detail or just feel an impression of a shape or color or feel. Whatever comes to you is fine. Feel the energy of your chosen angel/s and see it sweeping down your arm and into the crystal on your palm. Become aware of your crystal's vibration—it may feel like tiny pulses; it may be hot or cold. When you sense the vibration, you have the connection with your crystal.

* Say to yourself or aloud: "Blessed this crystal be." Now take a few minutes to really feel the energy of your angel–crystal link. Stay with this feeling as long as you wish.

* When you are ready to finish, thank your angels, open your eyes, and close down (see page 11). You might like to lay the crystal on your angel altar or carry it with you in a purse or bag, and touch it to connect with your angels. If you have dedicated your crystal to a particular archangel, know that this crystal will help you connect strongly

with that angel. For example, if you dedicate your stone to Archangel Michael, angel of freedom and protection, you could hold the crystal whenever you need to stand your ground.

ARCHANGELS AND THEIR CRYSTALS

Archangels also have particular crystal associations. Among them are:

* Michael—for truth, protection, and decisions: Deep yellow and purple stones including amber, golden topaz, diamond, clear quartz, and amethyst

* Gabriel—for dreams, messages, light, and guidance: Silver stones, including moonstone, mother of pearl, pearl, selenite, and opal

* Raphael—for healing and knowledge: Pale yellow and green stones, including citrine, emerald, yellow jasper, bloodstone, polished malachite, and green aventurine.

Did You Lose or Break a Crystal?

Crystals may break when their work is done. If this has happened, gather the pieces together and bury them in the earth, sending them back to their natural home.

If you lose a crystal you have had for a while, then you no longer need it. If you lose a crystal soon after you received it, then this stone wasn't for you. I (Liz) was once given a beautiful jade ring. I wore it just twice, and then it disappeared completely—although I knew it had to be somewhere in the house.

After searching everywhere, and later clearing out drawers to move home, I finally accepted that the vibration of jade just wasn't right for me at the time.

Angel Crystals

- **Celestite** (*blue*): The stone of heaven

- **Angel-wing calcite** (*white, lemon, wing-like formation*): The "angel-calling" stone

- **Angelite** (*blue and white*): The stone of awareness and truth

- **Aqua aura quartz** (*blue*): A channeling stone

- **Danburite** (*white*): A stone for peace and healing

- **Lemurian seed quartz** (*clear, smoky*): The lightworker's stone

- **Pink calcite:** Love and forgiveness

- **Rutilated quartz,** also known as angel-hair crystal (*clear, commonly with golden or brown threads*): The cosmic healer

- **Seraphinite** (*green*): A stone of enlightenment

- **Selenite** (*white*): A spiritual connection stone

(Some of these stones come in other colors, too—it is fine to use them.)

ALTERNATIVES

- **Clear quartz:** Known as the "master" crystal, because it magnifies and purifies energy

- **Rose quartz** (*shades of pink*): The love crystal

- **Amethyst** (*shades of purple*): For healing

7 A Crystal Ritual for Angelic Love

Angelic love is higher love—love that is selfless and kind, and universal and unconditional. To bring angelic love into your life and to find or strengthen a relationship, you can create a crystal love altar and call in the angel of love to help you.

The south-west is traditionally associated with attracting and strengthening love and relationships. Set up your altar in the south-west in a peaceful space in your home—this may be your bedroom or study, or a quiet corner of your living room.

You will need: a picture of an angel, or a figurine; a love crystal, such as rose quartz, rhodochrosite, kunzite, aventurine, or your dedicated angel crystal (see Tip 6); a pink candle.

The love ritual

* Find a quiet space to set up your love altar. Light the pink candle to symbolize the beginning of the ritual. Now go through the grounding, protection, and opening-up meditation (see pages 9–10). Hold a crystal in each palm, or one crystal with both hands, and begin to sense the vibration of your crystal. It may feel hot or cold, or you might feel a tingling in your palms, which shows you have connected with your crystal. Hold your crystal(s) throughout the meditation. You can sit comfortably in a chair, or lie down holding your crystals. If you lie down, you can place your crystal on your heart chakra. Experiment to find what feels best for you.

* Call upon your guardian angel, saying their name gently, then invite Haniel, an angel of love, to join you. When you tingle, or feel a shift in the energy around you—however you sense your angel's presence—you are ready to begin. Say: "Archangel Haniel, please bring love into my life. Thank you." Now choose one or more of the visualizations below.

* *For a new relationship:* If you are looking for a romantic relationship, set your intention. Visualize the face of your perfect man or woman. Give this imaginary picture as much detail as you can—hair color, smile, body shape. If you can't easily do this, just connect with the feeling of being totally in love. Breathe into this sensation or your picture, so the feeling of love expands and grows within you. You might sense this as your whole body filling with luminous pink light. Be aware of your crystal and feel its

energy pulsing as you visualize. Your crystal, with Archangel Haniel, energizes your intention to attract more love into your life. When you are ready, move on to the next ritual, or close down (see page 11), thanking your angels. Place your crystal(s) on your love altar.

For love from family and friends: Follow the ritual above, but this time visualize a group of friends and family joining hands, with Archangel Haniel standing behind them. Keep the focus on your breathing, seeing this breath as a conduit for love energy flowing from you to your circle of people and Archangel Haniel and back to you again. This breath is a ring of beautiful pink light, which expands to touch all the people you care about. Really feel this closeness and love, and feel this love imprinting on the crystals in your hands. Let your whole body feel the love vibration. When you are ready, move on to the next ritual, or close down (see page 11), thanking your angels. Place the crystal(s) on your love altar.

To send love to the planet: For earth healing, call upon Archangel Sandalphon, guardian of the earth, saying: "Archangel Sandalphon, please send love and healing to our planet. Thank you." As before, send out love energy with your breath. See the pink light swooping around the surface of Mother Earth, sending love to all its creatures. Feel your pure connection to the planet and the love you have for her. Sense the grounding in your feet, connecting you to the earth through deep, deep roots.

Stay with this feeling for as long as you like, still holding your crystals, and when you are ready, place them on the table or your angel altar as you gradually step back from the visualization. Thank your angels and Archangel Sandalphon, then close down (see page 11).

Whenever you want to reconnect with this feeling of pure, unconditional love, hold your crystals. They act as a portal to the special feelings you experienced in the meditation, which helps you make love a reality and manifest the love you want to give and to attract.

8 Connecting with Your Angels Through Color

When you begin to communicate with your angels, expand your intuition and experience your angels' presence through all your senses. When you make a request to your angels, the more feeling and connection you have, the more heartfelt and passionate your message, and the more your angels can hear you.

Working with color is one way to connect with your angels simply and instantly, and engages your right brain—the part of you responsible for dreams and imagination, unhindered by your logical left hemisphere. Try this protective visualization and talk to your angels with symbolic color.

THE ANGEL-WING MEDITATION

* Begin by sitting comfortably and closing your eyes. Ground, protect, and open up (see pages 9–10). When you are ready, ask your angels to come close, calling them by name and paying attention to your senses—the more you invite your angels to be with you, the more practiced you will become at sensing their presence through feeling pressure on your body, a tingling sensation, or a particular feeling of love and peace.

* Visualize your angel's wings and see them surrounding you, protecting you in a soft cocoon of feathers. This feels like sitting in a high-backed chair, fully surrounded by your angels' wings.

* Now choose a color (see below) and see it in your mind's eye; let it wash over your angel's wings. Let the color spread and deepen so that your angel glows with the energy of that color. Feel the color seep into you from your angel's feathers. If you would like more love in your life, visualize pink; for more energy, see your angel radiate yellow sunshine; for insight, let your angel's wings take on the color indigo.

* Sit with the image of your colored angel wings in your mind's eye. Feel your angel's love and joy at giving you this gift.

* When you are ready, thank your angel and close down (see page 11).

COLORS AND THEIR ANGELIC ASSOCIATIONS

Did you sense a color before you had a chance to visualize one? This shows that your angels are guiding you to focus on an issue in your life.

Red *is the color for Archangel Uriel.* He helps bring security, groundedness, and the ability to deal with change.

Orange *is Archangel Gabriel's color*, and relates to sexuality and self-expression.

Yellow *is for Archangel Jophiel*, for focus and energy, strength and joy.

Rose-pink, *the color of Archangel Haniel,* is for love, harmony, and compassion.

Green *is for Archangel Raphael*, who offers healing and protection.

Blue *is for Archangel Michael.* He helps you let go of fear and speak your truth.

Indigo *is for Archangel Raziel*, and intuition.

Violet *is for Archangel Zadkiel*, for transformation and spirituality.

White *is for Archangel Metatron*, for spiritual power; the angel of writers and the Akashic records, which is the library of our soul's incarnations.

For more colors, see Tip 24.

9 Wishing on an Angel when You're Dealing with Change

This strong angel meditation brings in red, the color associated with the base chakra, which is located at the base of the spine.

Red relates to your sense of identity, knowing who you are, and how secure you feel in life on all planes—physical, emotional, spiritual, financial. When things change, your security and identity can be challenged. Triggers for insecurity include meeting a new partner, moving home, gaining a promotion or changing career, losing a friend, traveling, illness, and losing or even inheriting money. Try this grounding meditation to help you feel secure and peaceful in yourself when everywhere around you seems to be in flux.

SECURITY MEDITATION: BASE CHAKRA

* To begin this exercise, first read the grounding, protection, and opening-up techniques on pages 9–10. This time, spend longer visualizing your grounding in detail: see tiny shoots sprout from your soles and grow thick and strong, burrowing deep into the earth's core through rich earth and small stones, then, at their deepest reach, finding huge crystal boulders. Give the boulders a color. Twine your roots around the rocks so you are completely anchored. Now let your roots bring the energy of the earth up to you; it is rising through the soles of your feet, through your ankles, and up your legs, then flowing up through the rest of your body to the crown of your head. Let this feeling be calm and restorative, knowing you are securely connected to the earth. Put on your protection bubble (see page 9) and open up to your angels (see page 10).

* Now invite in your angels, calling them by name, saying three times, aloud or to yourself: "My Angel, be with me and keep me safe." Thank your angel in advance for their help. Now begin to sense your angel's presence, if you have not already done so (with practice, you may feel your angel's presence as soon as you begin to ground and protect yourself at the beginning of a meditation). Feel the sensations on your skin, such as the brush of a hair against your face, or a gentle or strong tingling on your scalp or arm, or down one side of your body; everyone senses their angel's approach in a different way. Your angel's wings are around you, so you are almost enclosed by your angel's feathers, as if sitting in a high-backed chair with your angel's wings behind and above you, protecting you.

* Visualize the color red at the base of your spine (your base chakra; see the illustration on page 12) and see your angel's wings take on that color. Breathe slowly and deeply, enjoying the feeling of love and belonging as you connect with your angel and feel the grounding sensation of the color at the base of your spine. Stay attuned for as long as you need to, then, to end the meditation, come back to the sound of your breath, opening your eyes when you are ready.
* Close down your chakras (see page 11).

WHAT COLORS DID YOU SENSE?
When you visualized red, did you see a dark or a light red? Dark red with black, brown, or gray areas shows that you may be absorbing external negative energy. You can transform this by going back into the visualization and this time projecting a vibrant, pure shade of red into your base chakra to lift the vibration.

Did you see any other colors? Turn to the chart on page 39 to see what messages they hold.

HELP IN AN INSTANT
If you have only a little time, simply asking your angels to come close to you is enough to give you support. When you have developed a strong connection with your angels, this relationship will give you security and strength whenever you ask for it.

Angel to call upon:
- **Archangel Uriel**, angel of security

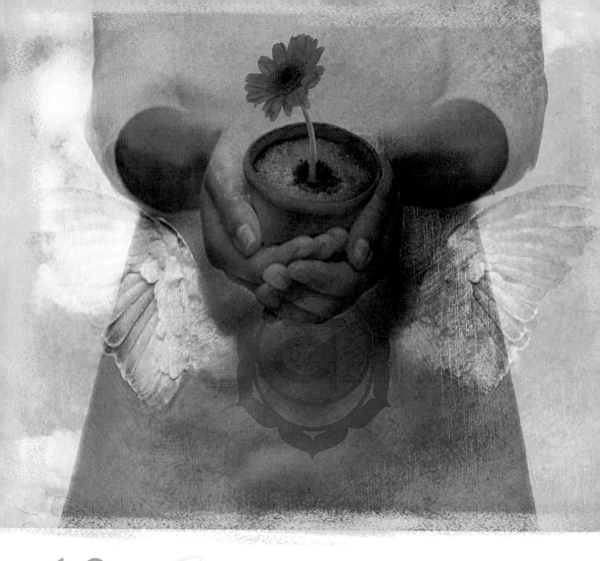

10 Wishing on an Angel for Fertility and Creativity

Orange empowers creativity, helping you manifest whatever you dream of. If your path to your dreams feels blocked, or if your projects need to speed up, this meditation can help.

Creativity Meditation: Sacral Chakra

* Begin by grounding, protecting, and opening up (see pages 9–10).
* Now call upon your angels to join you, wrapping their wings around you. Feel the feathers touch you as you sink deeply into a feeling of total protection and relaxation.
* Visualize swirling orange light around the area of your sacral chakra, cleansing and energizing (see the illustration on page 12). If you are trying to get pregnant, you can send the light around your womb and fallopian tubes.
* Let the orange light spread from you to your angels' wings, enclosing you. Let your thoughts rest on the project you want to develop or the child you would love to conceive. Visualize yourself having achieved this—you might see yourself with a finished business plan, or holding your baby. Say gently aloud or to yourself three times: "My Angels, please help me succeed in what I need. Thank you."
* You may also like to ask your angels to help remove any emotional blocks that may be obstructing you. If so, you can also call upon Archangel Gabriel, the angel of communication, to help you and your partner (if appropriate) express yourselves and release some of these feelings. Archangel Michael can also help you speak your truth and banish fear. If problems from the past may be getting in the way of conception, calling upon him can help break negative memories and thinking patterns that stop you moving forward in life.
* Stay with your angels' vibration as long as you like. When you are ready, open your eyes.
* Close down your chakras (see page 11).

WHAT COLORS DID YOU SENSE?

When you visualized orange, did you see a dark or a light orange? Dark orange with black, brown, or gray areas shows disruption to your "flow." You can transform this by going back into the visualization and this time projecting a vibrant, light orange into your sacral chakra to lift the vibration and clear the blocks.

Did you see other colors? Turn to the chart on page 39 to see what messages they hold.

Angels to call upon:

* **Archangel Gabriel,** angel of news, expression, and fertility; angel of the Annunciation
* **Lailah,** angel of conception
* **Archangel Haniel,** angel of love
* **Archangel Tzaphkiel,** the cosmic mother angel
* **Archangel Michael,** who cuts the ties that bind
* **Angel Cassiel,** for creativity

11 Wishing on an Angel for Strength and Joy

Try this angelic sun meditation when you need to boost your physical strength and regain your focus. You can also practice it to recoup your joie de vivre, reconnecting with your happy childhood self when you played in the sun without worrying about the past or the future.

Sun Meditation: Solar Plexus Chakra

* Follow the grounding, protection, and opening-up rituals (see pages 9–10).
* Now call upon your angel by name and begin to sense their approach: pay attention to your senses, tuning into any sensations that come to you, such as tingling on your skin or a change in temperature. When your angel feels close, say: "My Angel, please give me strength and energy, and bring back my light. Thank you." Say this gently aloud or to yourself three times. Let your angel's wings surround and comfort you. Visualize a sun in the area of your solar plexus chakra (see the illustration on page 12), glowing and pulsing as you grow in strength.
* Sit with this connection and stay attuned with your luminous angel for as long as you can; feel as if you are soaking up sunshine, restoring cells and organs. Sense how much you need—if you are feeling very low and depleted, you might wish to stay with this image for 10–15 minutes or more.

* Bring your focus back to your breath and see yourself exhaling tiredness as dullness and inhaling sunshine and angelic light. This symbolizes your self-cleansing and return to vitality. When you are ready, open your eyes.
* Close down your chakras (page 11), stretch, and walk a little, letting your renewed energy flow.

WHAT COLORS DID YOU SENSE?

With practice, you will sense your energy through color; sensing darkness or grayness around your solar plexus at the beginning of the visualization tells you you're in need of some angel strength! You can tap into this by going back into the visualization and this time projecting a vibrant, bright yellow into your solar plexus chakra to lift the vibration and clear the blocks.

Did you see any other colors? Turn to the chart on page 39 to see what messages they hold.

Angel to call upon:

• **Archangel Jophiel**, angel of strength

12 Wishing on an Angel for Healing

Green is the color of healing, and is also associated with the heart chakra and with love. Love heals, and with the loving help of your angels, you can ask for healing for yourself and also send healing to another person.

The Healing Angels Meditation: the Heart Chakra

* Follow the grounding, protection, and opening-up rituals (see pages 9–10).

* Now call upon the healing angels. The healing angels are a group led by Archangel Raphael, the holy healer. Invite them to step forward, and sense their wings behind you, enclosing you. You feel very safe.

* Feel the vibration of the healing angels. You might sense a pure white light flowing down from the crown of your head through your other six chakras—your third eye, throat, heart, solar plexus, sacral, and base (see the illustration on page 12). Now let this beautiful light expand into every part of you.

* You can ask the healing angels to give you whatever healing is needed, or be specific. You can ask by saying aloud or to yourself: "Healing angels, please help me with healing [this part of me/this condition]," and state the problem three times. Feel your angels' wings around you; see them blaze with white light. Stay with this vibration and really feel your angelic connection.

* When you are ready to finish, thank your healing angels and close down your chakras (see page 11).

WHAT COLORS DID YOU SENSE?

You may have sensed green, which is a healing color. Did you get pink? Pink and green are the colors of the heart chakra and the love vibration. Any darker areas in the colors you saw can show areas that your angels gave attention to, cleansing and lifting the vibrations there. You can also repeat the meditation, visualizing light pink and green to raise your vibration.

Did you see any other colors? Turn to the chart on page 39 to see what messages they hold.

HEALING A RIFT: SENDING YOUR ANGELS TO TALK TO THEIR ANGELS

You may like to call upon your angels to help heal a relationship. Harboring anger or sadness against someone takes your energy away and lowers your vibration. This simple ritual sends healing on an energetic level, raising the vibration between you and the other person. It's a really helpful option when other forms of communication have failed.

So, if you can't talk to this person, talk to your angels. Here's what to do:

* Ground, protect, and open up (see pages 9–10). Call upon your guardian angel, then ask the healing angel, Archangel Raphael, to join you, too, and Archangel Michael, for truth and communication.

* Visualize the person you need to contact. See their angels above them, and ask your angels to talk to their angels. Visualize your angels flying to their angels. Ask your angels to fix what needs to be fixed, so that you can reconcile or go your separate ways in peace. You don't need to ask for an outcome—just focus strongly on sending out your angels and see them talking to the other person's angels.

* Thank your angels and the other person for the positive things they have brought to your life. Now let go of the intention, and leave your angels to do their work.

* Close down your chakras (see page 11).

THE QUICK FORGIVENESS FIX

If you need to forgive yourself or another person, bring the image of the person into your heart center, and breathe in the pink light of love and compassion. Then exhale and visualize yourself breathing out any anger or hurt you are still feeling. Keep doing this, using your breath to set up an energy circuit between the two of you. Ask your angels to help you forgive yourself and the other person, and let go of the negative feelings. Thank your angels. If this person is destined to be a part of your future, your angels will help to reopen the lines of communication.

Angels to call upon:

• **Archangel Raphael,** the healing angel
• **Archangel Michael,** for communication
• **Archangel Sandalphon,** for distant healing and healing the earth

13 Wishing on an Angel for Love

Do you need more love in your life? Love is like water—it needs to flow and be shared. We often think love is just romantic, but the purest love is the love we know when connected to the Source—when feeling completely at one with everything.

This could be the moment you were sitting on a hill overlooking a bay, watching a gull float over the water. It might have been when you spent a day alone and felt really at home surrounded by all your possessions. People often cite one relationship when they talk about love—maybe it's when you held your child for the first time, or fell in love—but real love extends to all things and goes far beyond individual bonds; it's about being connected with the whole of life. And when you can feel that very special sense of belonging, all your relationships benefit.

In the love meditation opposite we visualize pink, the color of love, affection, and compassion;

it's common to see pink in the aura of someone who is in love, as pink is one of the colors of the heart chakra (see Tip 12).

The Love Meditation: Heart Chakra

* Ground and protect yourself, and open up (see pages 9–10).
* Invite your angel to join you, calling them by name. Ask your angel for love for yourself and others, saying gently aloud or to yourself: "My Angel, please bring love and guidance into my life." Do this three times, and really feel your positive intention in your heart and your breath.

Now you are connected with your angel, sense their wings glowing pink, and feel this beautiful color as a light in your heart chakra (see the illustration on page 12). Feel it glow, and let it soothe any angst or hurt. Feel the pink vibration around you, and feel at one with yourself and your angel. When you are ready, thank your angel, close down your chakras (see page 11), and open your eyes.

WHAT COLORS DID YOU SENSE?
If you saw pale pink, you are experiencing the highest love. Any dark areas and dark colors mixed with the pink, such as brown, gray, or black, can show past hurts you are holding on to. You can transform this by going back into the visualization and this time projecting a vibrant, pale pink into your heart chakra to lift the vibration there and to help clear any blocks.

Did you see any other colors? Turn to the chart on page 39 to see what messages they hold.

A QUICK WAY TO SEND LOVE TO OTHERS
When you have connected with your angels, visualize them sending pink light to the person or people you want to send love to. Thank your angels when this is done.

… AND TO RECEIVE LOVE FOR YOURSELF
Whenever you need a love boost, you need only ask your angel to come close. Simply being with your angel lets you experience pure, unconditional love. You can also practice the self-healing technique for heart healing (see Tip 34)—place your left hand on your higher heart chakra and your right hand on your solar plexus, and sense your angel's light filling you up.

Angels to call upon:

• **Archangel Haniel**, the love angel
• **Archangel Raphael**, the holy healer

14 *Wishing on an Angel for the Truth*

When you need to know the truth of a situation, talk to your angels. Blue is the color of truth—"true blue"—which you can bring into this revealing meditation.

THE TRUTH MEDITATION: THE THROAT CHAKRA

* Follow the grounding, protection, and opening-up ritual (see pages 9–10).
* Now invite your angels to come close. Really let yourself feel their loving vibrations. Check all your senses for tingling, heat and cold, taste, and aroma.
* Now feel your angels' wings around you, and encompassing your whole body. Sense a vibrant blue color wash over your angels' wings. Breathe slowly, following the sound of your breathing until you are ready to ask your angels to help you see the truth of a situation. But first, visualize the problem, so that your angels can see it, too. Give it as much detail as you can—sound, color, feeling.
* Call your angels by name, gently aloud or to yourself, saying: "My Angels, please tell me the truth about …" three times, and thanking them at the end of your request. Feel your angels' connection strongly as you do this, and focus on your feelings. Sense the answer to your question within you.
* When you are ready to finish, close down your chakras (see page 11).

* You can ask your angels to give you confirmation that the answer is correct. Look out for angel signs (see Tip 1)—they will be there for you.

THE LITTLE BLUE ANGEL

You can carry a little blue angel or any blue crystal with you when you feel you need clarity and sense you might not be getting the whole story. Keep your blue angel close when you're in a difficult meeting at work, or whenever truth is really important—when you're having problems communicating in personal relationships, for instance. Sometimes you can feel blocked and can't say what you want to say because others are putting up barriers. Hold your blue angel and ask him to show you the truth.

THE QUICK COMMUNICATION UPGRADE

To communicate better with people around you and with your angels, follow the ritual above, focussing on your throat (this is the location of your throat chakra, which is linked with the color blue; see the illustration on page 12). Ask your angels to clear communication blocks, and for the confidence to express your feelings and opinions.

WHAT COLORS DID YOU SENSE?

Vibrant blues in the upgrade visualization—from heaven-blue to lighter shades—show high-level communication. Very dark blue and dark colors mixed with the blue, such as brown, gray, or black, can show issues you need to voice. You can transform this energy by going back into the visualization and this time sending a vibrant blue beam of light into your throat chakra to lift the vibration there and help you speak your truth.

Did you see any other colors? Turn to the chart on page 39 to see what messages they hold.

Angels to call upon:

- **Archangel Michael**, angel of truth and communication
- **Archangel Gabriel**, angel of messages and revelations

15 *Wishing on an Angel for Insight and Intuition*

Your angels can guide you on your spiritual path, helping you trust your intuition. The process of talking to your angels regularly helps you trust yourself and your feelings—this alone will help you in many areas of your life.

How many times have you kicked yourself for ignoring your instincts because it wasn't convenient? We often put off resolving a problem or relationship regardless of the inner voice that's saying *Don't do it: Walk away: Do it …* because this involves risk. But once ignored, the same situation or problem simply reappears, perhaps in another guise, until you do follow your intuition.

In this way, trusting yourself completely can be a challenge. It can also be difficult on a day-to-day basis, particularly if you sense things that others don't always experience. You might think, "Is what I'm getting here just my imagination? Or is it real?" The answer is that visualization opens up intuition. That is, you need your sensitivity and imagination to become receptive to intuitive flashes and messages from your angels, but the messages themselves are "real." Think about it this way. If you were to visualize making a bowl from clay, you would use your imagination to visualize its shape and form, to make it by hand, and to

decorate it beautifully. When the bowl is fired (with your positive intentions), it is ready to use. Your angels now have a bowl, a place, to leave messages for you. You needed to make the bowl with your imagination and intention in order to collect the messages.

With practice, you will come to recognize the transition point from imagination into new territory. During an angel meditation, for example, you begin by using your imagination to become receptive—grounding yourself by seeing roots growing from your feet, and placing yourself in a protective bubble. But when you call upon your angels and sense their presence, this is not something you have willed into being. Angels are all about feeling, not willpower and determination. That is why trying too hard to see your angels can often mean that you won't; but by being relaxed and receptive, and trusting your intuition, you create a pathway for your angels to visit.

Intuition meditation: Third—Eye Chakra

* To ask your angels to boost trust and intuition, first ground and protect yourself and do the opening-up ritual (see pages 9–10).
* Now visualize an indigo pathway. Indigo is the color of intuition and the third-eye chakra (see the illustration above). The pathway begins at your third eye, between your eyebrows, and extends out into the sky. See your angels walking along this path towards you. Let the color become more vibrant as your angels come closer. They are bringing you beautiful indigo light. Thank your angels in advance of your meeting.
* When you are ready, let your angels wrap their wings around you. They are also purple, and you feel this color vibrate at your third eye.
  Your angels are telling you that they trust you, and now it is time to trust yourself. Your intuition is real.

* Stay with this loving vibration as long as you like.
* When you are ready to finish, thank your angels once more and close down your chakras (see page 11).

WHAT COLORS DID YOU SENSE?

Sensing lots of indigo—in this meditation and others—shows that the angels are helping you cleanse old energies and lift your vibration. Your intuition is expanding and becoming stronger. Did you find it difficult to "see" indigo? If you sensed other colors, turn to page 39 to find out their associations. These are the issues you might consider working on in order to trust your intuition more deeply.

Angels to call upon:

* **Archangel Raziel**, angel of intuition
* **Archangel Barachiel**, angel of insight, imagination, and psychic development

16 Wishing on an Angel for Spiritual Development

If you are developing your ability to link with the spiritual realms, your angels can help you strengthen your connection. You can ask them to teach you—angels love to help you along your path.

Before you begin this meditation, work with the intuition chakra (see Tip 15), because intuition is your link with clairvoyant experience. Clairvoyance is "clear-seeing," when you receive messages from the spiritual realms as images. Some people may be more clairsentient—feeling sensations in your body, such as tingling, changes of temperature, or your hair being stroked when your angels are close. If you hear messages, it is likely you're clairaudient. Many people who talk with angels receive messages in more than one way, but as a term, clairvoyance has generally come to encompass many of these sensory experiences.

In this meditation, white is the color of connection with Source energy, or the divine. White is also the color of the crown chakra (it can also be seen as violet), located on the crown of your head, and this is the part of your body that connects directly with the realm of spirit and the angels. When you connect yourself to the Source during meditation, you open up to receive messages from your angels.

The Spiritual Path Meditation: The Crown Chakra

* Begin by grounding and protecting yourself, and opening up (see pages 9–10)—breathing your energy up from the roots of the earth, through the base, sacral, solar plexus, heart, throat, and third eye chakras, and right up to the crown (see the illustration on page 12), then breathing in pure white light at the crown, which flows back down through your chakras, filling your body with light.

* Now turn your attention to your crown chakra. Focus on the angelic white light pouring into your crown. Sense your crown chakra as a spinning wheel or a flower that is opening. See the wheel get bigger and stronger or the flower petals opening fully.

* Call in your angels, saying three times: "My Angels, be with me, help me on my path," then focus again on your breathing. Notice any sensations you feel and any images that come in.

* You might see action you need to take, or receive predictive messages during this meditation—a strong feeling of knowing about future events or sensing these events in pictures. (If so, write down your observations straight away, just in note form, in your angel journal—see Tip 19, page 62).

* When you are ready to finish the meditation, close down (see page 11). It is important to remember to do this, particularly when you have been working with the crown chakra, because if you leave yourself open you can absorb into your energy field unwanted emotions—the pain, hopes, thoughts, and experiences of others.

* Thank your angels and trust that they will take care of you. Know that they will watch over you and bring in the right spiritual opportunities when you are ready.

WHAT COLORS DID YOU SENSE?

If you sensed colors, turn to page 39 to find out their associations. If these colors were clear, light, and vibrant, the angels were showing you your strengths. Any dull or dark colors relate to areas to work on; these can become your strengths and help you grow spiritually.

Angel to call upon:

• **Archangel Metatron**, angel of spirituality

17 What's your Astro-Angel?

Each astrological sign has its own ruling angel, whom you can call upon to reinforce your positive qualities, empowering you whenever you need a stronger sense of self. You can connect with your astro-angel at any time of year, not just during your birthday month. Below are listed the twelve signs and their angels, the qualities they offer you, and the special color each angel radiates.

To talk to your astro-angel, ground and protect yourself (see pages 9–10), and ask for a connection by calling their name three times and visualizing their color. Three is the number of magic and creation. You can also wear your zodiac or month-angel's color to empower your connection. (For crystals, incense, and flower associations, see pages 32, 80, and 102.)

MAKING AN ANGELIC CONNECTION WITH ANOTHER ASTRO-SIGN

Can you cosmically connect? Try this ritual on a Friday, as this is the day ruled by Archangel Haniel, one of the angels of love. If you can, do it during a waxing moon phase—this is when the moon is growing into a full moon (you can check when the moon is waxing on an astrology or astronomy website).

* Place two candles on your altar, one of your astro-sign color, and one for the other person's, or take two crystals—again, your astro-crystal and the crystal representing the other person's astro sign—one in each hand. Ask the angel of the moon and guidance, Archangel Gabriel, to guide you together if this should be your destiny, and Archangel Haniel to help your relationship grow. Then place both crystals together on your altar. If you are using candles, light them both, make the same request, and thank these angels for their help. Blow out the candles and leave the candles and/or crystals on your altar for a moon cycle of 28 days. Within this time you should have your answer.

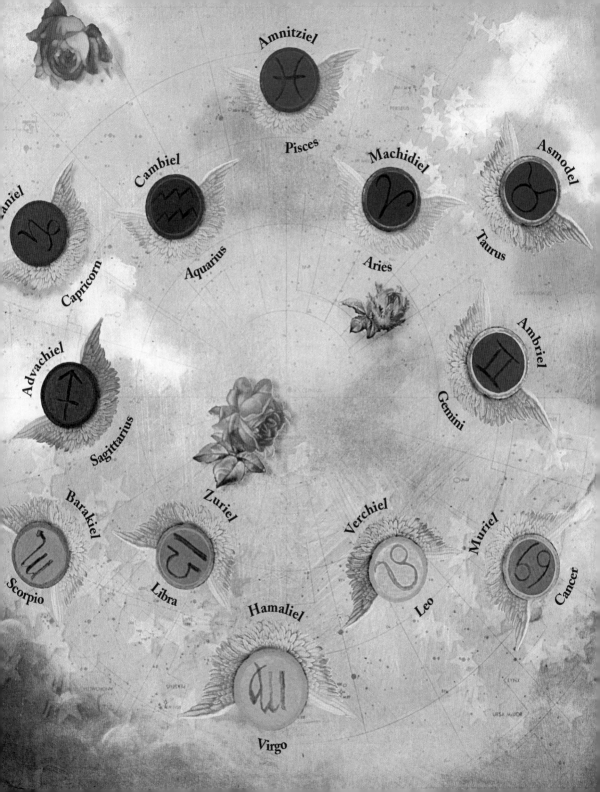

Amnitziel

Pisces

Cambiel

Aquarius

...aniel

Capricorn

Advachiel

Sagittarius

Barakiel

Zuriel

Scorpio

Libra

Hamaliel

Virgo

Machidiel

Aries

Asmodel

Taurus

Ambriel

Gemini

Verchiel

Muriel

Leo

Cancer

ARIES

21 March–20 April

Angel Machidiel

- SYMBOL: The ram
- ANGEL MACHIDIEL'S GIFTS: Self-belief, focus, drive, action
- COLOR: Red
- CRYSTALS: Carnelian, diamond, Herkimer diamond

TAURUS

21 April–21 May

Angel Asmodel

- SYMBOL: The bull
- ANGEL ASMODEL'S GIFTS: Loyalty, luxury, patience, resourcefulness
- COLOR: Red-orange
- CRYSTALS: Rose quartz, emerald

GEMINI

22 May–21 June

Angel Ambriel

- SYMBOL: The twins
- ANGEL AMBRIEL'S GIFTS: Communication, flexibility, openness
- COLOR: Orange
- CRYSTALS: Citrine

CANCER

22 June–22 July

Archangel Muriel

- SYMBOL: The crab
- ANGEL MURIEL'S GIFTS: Sensitivity, caring, keeping secrets
- COLOR: Amber
- CRYSTALS: Moonstone, pearl

LEO

23 July–23 August

Angel Verchiel

- SYMBOL: The lion
- ANGEL VERCHIEL'S GIFTS: Leadership, vision, generosity, courage
- COLOR: Lemon-yellow
- CRYSTALS: Golden topaz, tiger's eye

VIRGO

24 August–22 September

Angel Hamaliel

- SYMBOL: The maiden
- ANGEL HAMALIEL'S GIFTS: Organization, relationships, healing
- COLOR: Yellow-green
- CRYSTALS: Jade, peridot, moss agate

LIBRA

23 September–23 October

Angel Zuriel

- SYMBOL: The scales
- ANGEL ZURIEL'S GIFTS: Harmony, justice, brain-power
- COLOR: Emerald
- CRYSTALS: Lapis lazuli, sodalite, blue topaz

SCORPIO

24 October–22 November

Archangel Barachiel

- SYMBOL: The scorpion
- ANGEL BARACHIEL'S GIFTS: Intuition, chance, intensity, spirituality
- COLOR: Green-blue
- CRYSTALS: Obsidian, coral, aqua aura

SAGITTARIUS

23 November–21 December

Angel Advachiel

- SYMBOL: The archer
- ANGEL ADVACHIEL'S GIFTS: Travel, creativity, perspective
- COLOR: Blue
- CRYSTALS: Ruby, turquoise

CAPRICORN

22 December–20 January

Archangel Haniel

- SYMBOL: The goat
- ANGEL HANIEL'S GIFTS: Steadfastness, honesty, financial management
- COLOR: Indigo
- CRYSTALS: Garnet, ruby

AQUARIUS

21 January–18 February

Archangel Cambiel

- SYMBOL: The water-carrier
- ARCHANGEL CAMBIEL'S GIFTS: Communication, revelation, messages
- COLOR: Orange
- CRYSTALS: Moonstone, mother of pearl, opal

PISCES

19 February–20 March

Angel Amnitziel

- SYMBOL: The fish
- ANGEL AMNITZIEL'S GIFTS: Empathy, originality
- COLOR: Crimson
- CRYSTALS:- Bloodstone, fluorite, coral

18 Making an Angel Altar

Dedicating a special space in your home for your angels, no matter how small, creates a physical place to meet with your celestial friends. From the end of a mantelpiece to a corner of a living room, a square foot of your yard to a whole room for your angel figurines, any space you dedicate raises the vibrations of your entire home.

Look through any angel items you have. What do you love most? Set aside favorite angel figurines, wings, cherubs, and fresh or silk flowers, along with candles in your favorite colors, or the colors of the angels you would like to communicate with (see Tip 8). Angels are connected with crystals, too, and have their own associated stones—but you can place any crystals you would like to work with in your angel space. Crystals including seraphinite, angelite, celestite, selenite, rutilated quartz, and angel aura quartz are high-vibration, and help make a link with the angelic realms (see Tip 6). Add some angel incense and/or an aromatherapy oil burner and essential oils (see Tip 26).

Before you arrange your offerings, clear and clean the space thoroughly, and open the nearest window or door to let fresh air flow. Next, you can mist (see Tip 27)—add two drops of lavender essential oil and two drops of sage essential oil to about 1 fl. oz. (30ml) spring water; lavender neutralizes any negative vibes and sage cleanses, helping to make your angelic connection fast and clear. (If you are pregnant, it is best to avoid handling these oils.)

MAKING AN ABUNDANCE ALTAR

You can give an altar any theme. Abundance is perfect, because it embodies prosperity of heart, mind, and pocket, too.

* First make an Angel Mist with two drops of peppermint oil, three drops of spearmint oil, and three drops of lavender oil diluted in about 1 fl. oz. (30ml) spring water. Then gather together some objects that symbolize abundance. You could add a small pile of coins, pretty items in gold or silver, and some favorite crystals—if you have pyrite and citrine, all the better, as they attract money and abundance. Add a picture of what you would like to have—be realistic, though, as your angels will respond to need rather than complete fantasy!

WHAT TO AVOID PLACING ON YOUR ALTAR
Consider how your altar treasures came to you. If you are framing angel greetings cards, who did they come from? Is the sender someone you are still in touch with, and like? If you sense any negative attachment to any item, do not place it on your altar. Only display items that you love, and that have happy, loving associations for you.

Refresh your altar each week, dusting and cleaning figurines, crystals, candles, and pictures to keep the energy of this special space fresh, the pathways of communication clear, and the vibration high.

BLESSING YOUR ANGEL ALTAR
Say three times: "I dedicate this space to my angels so they may talk with me. May this space be our place for all that is love."

Thank your angels.

19 Keeping an Angel Journal

Connecting with angels is not a finite process. Once you are connected, your relationship can blossom—just like earthly relationships. Your angel journal records the positive changes that angelic connection brings.

The more you work with your angels, the more sensitive you become to their energies (and to the energies of the people in your life). Your compassion grows, and it becomes easier to love and to forgive. Also, reflect on your relationship with yourself. Are you finding it easier to be more compassionate toward yourself now that you are working with your angels? You may find that you don't give yourself as hard a time when things go wrong, and that you're able to step back from a situation and see the bigger picture. Are you finding it easier to let go? Do you just "know" things for no reason, generally feel stronger in your beliefs, and have more direction?

Your angel journal is the place to express all these inspiring changes.

Dedicate a journal just for you and your angels. You could note:

* Angels in your dreams
* Angel occurrences
* Earth Angels—when strangers help (see Tip 23)
* Your angel card readings (see Tip 39)
* Your angel wishes, with dates
* Outcomes, intuition, impressions
* Words and sketches
* Colors
* Ideas for stories and projects

GRATITUDE

Include a gratitude section at the back of your journal. Each night, write down three things to be thankful for. Try to write down something, even if it's small: for being warm, for a friend at the end of the phone, for your affectionate dog/cat, or just for it not raining! This gratitude practice shifts your mood at the end of a difficult day, and reinforces the positives after a good day.

However your angels help you in life, keeping a journal tracks your developing relationship. As you recognize your important connection with your angels, you evolve spiritually and begin to get more information and messages during meditations, visualizations, angel rituals, and dreams.

20 _Make an Angel Vision Board_

A vision board is a special arrangement of images that is displayed on your angel altar (see Tip 18) or in another prominent place in your home. It helps you set an intention to attract all the good things you want in life, from a new home to more friends, a relationship, or to travel the world.

You can create virtually any possibility for yourself with just a basic picture frame, old magazines, scissors, glue—and the help of your guiding angels.

* Start by placing a picture of an angel or some angel wings in the center of the board of a picture frame. Or you could take a feather from your altar and build your vision board around that. By placing your angel in the center, you are symbolically making him the center of your wishes, or manifesting, and asking for his help to make your wishes come true.

* Next, cut out images of the things you would like to bring into your life. These can be objects or metaphors—for example, if you would like things to flow better—such as money, work, or love—an image of a flowing river would be perfect. Focus on how you want to feel when you have your wishes, rather than just thinking about attaining the objects or goals. Angels connect with the high vibration

of happiness, so try to project this feeling when you are busy putting your images together. Feel the joy, as if you already have these things.

* When you have finished making your vision board, tune in to your angels by grounding, protecting, and opening up (see pages 9–10), and ask your angels to help you work toward your goals. Thank them for their help, and let go of the wish, happy in the knowledge that your angels are taking care of your request.

* Close down (see page 11).

21 *Write an Angel Blessing or a Letter*

Angel blessing scrolls are messages written on small pieces of paper and rolled into a tiny scroll. You write down your request to your angel, then place the blessing scroll on your altar for seven days, or sleep with it under your pillow for seven nights. Seven is a mystical number and the number of creation, helping your wish manifest.

Before you begin, tune in to your angels, remembering to ground and protect yourself first (see pages 9–10). Visualize your angels' wings around you (see the angel-wing meditation in Tip 8), and, if you have one, hold a crystal you have dedicated to angel communion, such as rose quartz or angel-wing calcite (see Tip 6). You may like to

connect with your guardian angel or simply ask your angels in general to gather round you as you write your request. Whatever you do, begin when you feel a connection, and write from the heart.

HOW TO WRITE YOUR MESSAGE

* Dedicate the little paper scroll and pen you will write with to angelic work. Hold them in your right hand, connect with your angels, and say: "I dedicate these tools for working with my angels." Feel the connection as a light passing from the angelic realm down through the crown of your head, through your third eye, throat, and heart chakras (see page 12), then through your right arm and hand, and into the pen and scroll. You have a manifesting chakra on the palm of each hand, and when you dedicate tools or dedicate and activate crystals by holding them, you link this chakra with your angels, bringing down their energy as you desire.

* As you hold the pen, focus on the vibration of your angels. Now set your intention. Imagine that your wish has been granted.

* Write the blessing as if your wish has already been granted. This might be:

  "My angels, my mother is feeling much better …"

  "My angels, thank you for bringing more money to us …"

  "My angels, I now have a great job …"
* As you write, let the pen flow freely over the paper, sensing how your angels are with you and guiding you.
* Thank your angels, and sign the blessing with the name you are legally known by—not a nickname or other abbreviation. This is a formal request!
* Write the words "Blessing granted."
* Roll up the scroll and tie it with ribbon or similar—the prettier it looks, the better, as angels love color and beauty.
* Place it on your altar.

Let the angels do the rest.

Angel to call upon:
• **Archangel Metatron**, the celestial scribe.

E—MAIL YOUR BLESSINGS
This is very easy and effective. Just follow the instructions above, but this time write an e—mail to your angels with your request, remembering to write as if your wish has been granted. Write the wish three times, finishing with your full name and adding "Blessing granted." Then write "Thank you, My Angels." Now e—mail it to yourself. If you have an angel-minded friend, you can e—mail your requests to her, and ask her to e—mail it back to you. Ask her to do the same. By reading, e—mailing, and exchanging your requests, you are empowering your intention that your wish is granted.

TWEET A BLESSING
Here's how you can use Twitter to send out a request to your angels. Tweet your blessing to @psychicsisters. Every week, Jayne and her team at Psychic Sisters gather together to ask their angels to help make your wishes come true.

Signing off with an archangel

If there's a particular archangel whom you'd like to empower your blessing or letter, write the name of this angel after "Blessing granted." Choose an angel linked with your message theme - such as Haniel, for love; Raphael, to send healing; or Michael, for truth and protection. See the Angel Directory on page 136 for more archangels and their associations.

22 Dream Angels

Do you dream of angels? Vivid colors, angels, wings, and luminous, otherworldly forms have been sent to us in dreams for centuries, from the biblical Joseph, whose dream angel told him to marry Mary, to the visions and dreams of religious mystics such as Hildegard von Bingen and Joan of Arc.

Angels have influenced some of our most respected writers and artists, including Dante Alighieri, John Milton, and William Blake. Blake, the English poet, painter, and visionary, believed that he saw angels in his dreams, and all around him. For him, and for many angel healers and "seers," angels appear in visions in everyday life, taking the leap from the stuff of dreams into reality. At the age of just nine, near his home in Peckham Rye, south London, Blake saw "a tree filled with angels, bright angelic wings bespangling every bough like stars."

Angels can come to us in dreams and visions as messengers, to offer guidance, insight, and ways to solve a problem. Most of the time you may not remember your angels' presence in your dreams, only that you felt something deeply; maybe the colors in your dream were very vivid and beautiful. When you awake, you feel calmer and happier than usual. The angels may have given you a solution or idea!

PROPHETIC ANGEL DREAMS

Angels may visit in dreams to herald a big event. This "future event" dream will feel incredibly intense (but never frightening), and may wake you up. If this happens, stay with the feeling of the dream and let its sensations drift into your waking consciousness. Your angel has delivered a suitcase of sensations and messages to you in your sleep, and now it's time for some gentle unpacking.

* Take your angel journal (see Tip 19) and write down your first impressions or record them on your phone. Make a note of the date. Recall any aromas, signs, and symbols in your dream, and feel their impact on you. Try to stay with the feeling of the dream as you let these sensations flow.

* You can also take some angel message cards or any angel cards you like to work with and keep them by your bed. After a dream, choose a card from the deck as soon as you begin to wake up. This card will hold a message from your dream angels.

Some Dream Messages

* Flying (not fearful but blissful): Your angels are giving you an education, showing you the world and perhaps the cosmos. You are developing spiritually. It's time to do more and follow your path.
* People from the past: Your angels are showing you relationships that need healing or attention. Your angels are showing you these people without judgment. They may be asking you, too, to drop your judgment about a person or yourself in the events you saw in your dream.
* Insecurity dreams. These are common, and include:
* Losing something, such as an important document or your purse
* Being late for an appointment, or missing a train or airplane
* Walking around in public half-dressed
* Teeth falling out
* Falling or sinking
* Failing a test
* Being chased
* Being trapped
* Car trouble, or faults with technology, such as your phone breaking

In these dreams, your mind is processing fears and worries. This fear can block your connection with your angels, so you may be being asked to work on these issues. If you experience these dreams a lot, ask your guardian angel to hold your hand before you go to sleep and help you relax.

Archangel Gabriel is the angel of dreams and messages. Along with angel Auriel, he is one of the angels of the moon.

MOON MAGIC

If you received an angel sensation in your dream without any specific events or messages, you may have been visited by the angel of the Moon Day. An angel governs each day of the moon's 28-day cycle. Work out the day of your dream according to the moon's cycle—you can look this up on astronomy or astrology websites—then see the table opposite for the message.

The second part of the moon cycle, days 14–28, is the waning phase, when the full moon decreases to no moon. Energy wanes, so there are fewer positive attributes here, although there are still some highlights: day 22 links with healing and freedom, day 27 with prosperity, and day 28 with love and friendship.

HOW DO I KNOW IF MY DREAM WAS AN ANGEL DREAM?

Hans Christian Andersen's story "Holger Danske" (1845) tells of the eponymous sleeping hero, who dreams of everything that is happening in

Angel Messages and the Lunar Cycle

DAY	MESSAGE	ANGEL
1	Good journeys	Geniel
5	Health and protection, travel	Gabriel
7, 8, 10, 14, 28	Love and friendship	Scheliel
		Amnediel
		Ardifiel
		Ergediel
		Amnitziel
11, 13, 15, 17, 27	Improving prosperity	Neciel
		Jezeriel
		Atliel
		Adriel
		Atheniel
22	Healing, freedom	Geliel

Denmark. Every Christmas Eve an angel comes from God to tell him that all his dreams are true.

If you doubt your dreams, ask your angels for a message of reassurance. Did you find a tiny feather by your front door the morning after your dream? This is just one of the signs (see Tip 1) that your angels are with you, guiding you in your dreams at night and walking by your side each day.

You might also like to try the dream technique in Tip 44 (Five special angels/Gabriel).

23 Earth Angels: When Angels Send People to Help You

Earth Angels are angels who have been incarnated as humans to help us and the planet. There are many Earth Angels among us, quietly getting on with their work. We use the word "angel" all the time as a term of endearment for someone who is good, kind, and loving. At some level, we are all acknowledging that angels are already among us.

There are hundreds of stories of Earth Angel intervention—the cabdriver who appears in a no-go zone during a city bombing and rescues a stranded commuter, minutes before a devastating explosion; the lone walker who directs a carful of lost tourists, but then strangely disappears into the mist; the road worker who pushes a mother and her stroller out of the path of a parked truck that begins to move.

What connects these stories and many more like them is not just incredible happenstance, but that after their ordeals are over, no one can really remember what their good Samaritan looked like or explain how they came to be in the right place at the right time. Virtually everything about them is magically forgotten. And it's only after the fact that the truth dawns. Talking through the incident an hour afterward, or even years later, it's obvious that the impossible really happened. How did that stranger appear from nowhere and know exactly what to do?

Another common thread to these stories is that we accept the help of the Earth Angel without question. Nothing feels odd or threatening—it seems entirely natural to accept their help. We probably thanked them at the time, or turned around to thank them for saving us after a traumatic event, only to find that they had disappeared. Their work was done.

So whenever you get help from a stranger you can't remember, it means your angels are looking after you, keeping you on your path.

MESSAGES FROM EARTH ANGELS YOU KNOW

Your angels may also designate ordinary people to be your temporary Earth Angels. Earth Angels can be the least likely people. The angels choose as your Earth Angel the person who is best able to give you the message or help you in your life, regardless of their history with you. In this story, the angels chose a "problem" person to be Geri's Earth Angel, to show her that they had heard her prayer:

"My daughter told me she wanted to invite her father, my ex-husband, to my granddaughter's christening and asked if I would mind. I had not seen my ex for some years. As he could be a very difficult man, I wouldn't exactly relish seeing him,

but for her sake I agreed. Even though they had a somewhat fractured relationship, I knew my daughter really wanted him to come, perhaps as some sort of healing process.

"Instead of worrying about it, I decided to ask the angels to help. I concentrated on my guardian angel and my ex-husband's guardian angel, and asked them if they could work it out on a higher level.

"Later on, at the christening, our paths crossed—and that's when he looked me in the eyes and opened his mouth to say 'Hello Geraldine … I am an angel.' Then he suddenly continued with a completely different conversation, as if he hadn't even realized he had spoken those words. It was not the usual type of thing he would say, either—it was as if his angel was speaking through him, letting us know they really were working on it!"

ANIMALS CAN BE YOUR HEALING EARTH ANGELS

Angels can communicate with us through animals, to bring love and healing, as this experience from Jen shows:

"Our beloved cat, Sasha, had been with us—me and my husband, Brian—for 17 years. We'd had her as a kitten when we bought our first house together. She was a dainty little tortoiseshell, with a feisty streak—she'd see off bigger cats and even dogs if necessary.

"Sasha confronted a much larger dog one night, who decided to 'play' back with a swipe, leaving her covered in blood on the sidewalk near our house. The dog's owner ran to help, but the shock for an elderly feline such as Sasha was too much. She passed away before his eyes. He wrapped her in a blanket and knocked at our door, in tears at what had happened.

"That night, I asked my angels for comfort. I could barely sleep and I'd been crying for hours, ever since her little body was brought back to the house. I must have dropped off eventually, but I remember waking up at 4am to find our other cat, Luggy, a large ginger tom who never came into the bedroom, snuggling up to me. He was lying in exactly the same position that Sasha lay each night—in the crook of my ankles. At first I thought it was Sasha, and for a moment forgot that she had died. But no—the horrible reality of Sasha's death jolted me back to reality. This was Luggy.

"I looked down at him. He isn't the brightest of creatures compared to clever Sasha—he never knows which door of the house to come in, and he is terrified of other cats. But his long ginger fur

was glowing green, bright green. His eyes flashed and his fur pumped out heat, warming me just as Sasha had. I felt a sort of glow in my heart chakra when I stroked him.

"After that night, I slept better. The pain of losing Sasha eased a little every time my 'green' cat, Luggy, came to sleep in my bed, and whenever I stroked him. It was as if the angels gave me a little bit of Sasha back whenever I needed her."

24 Shine with the Archangel Colors

Connecting with your angels through color raises your vibration. When your vibration is high, you are full of energy—literally buzzing—and you open to a world of optimism and possibility.

You know you can ask your angels for anything, and that your angels love and support you whatever you do. You also attract others with a higher vibration. If you're feeling low and depleted, or you're on a vibration "high" and want to keep the vibration going, give yourself a beautiful energy boost with the archangel colors.

THE COLORS OF THE ARCHANGELS
Wearing the colors of the archangels lifts your mood and vibration. You can wear a little (or a lot) of the color of the angels you want to connect with, or display some of your angels' colors in your home. Angels love luminous, joyful hues. If you've got into the habit of donning black nearly every day of the working week because it's winter, it's cold, and you prefer the anonymity on public transport, make a vow not to wear black for just one week. Observe the impact this has on your mood and interaction with others—you may find yourself getting more attention, and feeling more vibrant. Color is energy, and when you change your colors, you influence your personal vibration. The higher your vibration, the more you can resonate with the heavenly vibration of your angels.

Traditionally, archangel colors link with the seven colors of the rainbow, as follows:

- **White:** *Archangel Metatron*, for divine communication
- **Yellow:** *Archangel Jophiel*, for energy and wisdom
- **Pink:** *Archangel Haniel*, for love
- **Red:** *Archangel Uriel*, for wisdom
- **Green:** *Archangel Raphael*, for healing
- **Blue:** *Archangel Michael*, for truth and protection
- **Orange:** *Archangel Gabriel*, for creativity and fertility
- **Violet:** *Archangel Zadkiel*, for spiritual growth
- **Indigo:** *Archangel Raziel*, for insight and intuition
- **Turquoise:** *Archangel Haniel*, for higher love
- **Lilac:** *Archangel Tzaphkiel*, for angelic guidance

(For the full listing of archangel associations, see the Directory, page 136.)

25 Asking the Parking Angel for a Parking Space

The parking angel deserves a special mention, as this is one of the angels most frequently called on—for obvious reasons! You might ask for a parking space once, twice, three times a week when you're late for a meeting, trying to park in a busy city, or have children or heavy goods to carry and need to be as close to your destination as you can.

The parking angel is Ambriel, but asking simply for the "parking angel" will do just fine. If you need help generally with traveling, call upon Archangel Michael (see below).

* As you're driving, ask for a space and imagine parking in an instant. Thank the parking angel in advance, look for a space, and see one appear. You can hang a tiny paper or crystal angel from your mirror as a reminder that your parking angel will always try to help you. Jayne has a tiny angel hanging over her mirror, and when she needs to park, she says, "Please park me!" and holds it for a second if it's safe to do so.

You can use any crystal or an angel figurine to represent your parking angel. Before you use it in the car, hold it gently, close your eyes, and dedicate it to helping you with parking (or any other issue with your car or driving). Keep holding it until you feel the crystal's vibration in the palms of your hands, which means that your angels and your crystal or figurine are connected. Hang the figurine over your mirror, or place the crystal in the glovebox or door pocket. You can add a piece of tiger's eye or rutilated quartz to give you and your vehicle protection.

ARCHANGEL MICHAEL, WHO HELPS YOU WITH TRAVELING

Archangel Michael protects your journeys, so you can call upon him whenever you are suffering from travel stress—delays, traffic congestion, or being overladen with things to carry—but you can also ask him to ensure a smooth journey before you set off. Imagine him by your side, wearing blue robes, and carrying his sword of protection, helping you on your way. Say thank you, release the connection, then begin your journey.

26 *Angels and their Aromas*

When you connect with angels, you might sense an aroma that tells you your angels are present. Many people report these angelic scents as having natural floral or herbal notes. You may find the aroma is very delicate. It is never synthetic, or unpleasant.

You might be able to detect an aroma for one of your angels. Angels, like people, have different energies, and bring with them different gifts: some come with music (see Tip 42), others with intense light and color; your guardian angel may simply touch your hair, or he may leave another sign for you.

If you have an angel that brings an aroma, what do you feel? Do you see a flower that comes with the fragrance? This can be your angel showing you its color and scent. A feeling of deep peace and the color white can tell you your peace angels are with you. Peace angels are a heavenly group that work together to bring peace to the world. When I (Liz) connect with them, I get the fragrance of sandalwood.

Sensing Other Beings in Spirit

If you detect other scents while you are connected, one of your spirit guides may be near. Tobacco smoke is very common when a guide is bringing through in spirit a loved one who used to smoke; or you might recognize a particular feminine scent, such as rose or lavender, which may signify an older female relative who has passed on and is now present to you in spirit. Angels love floral smells, too, but you might distinguish between an angelic scent and a spirit-guide scent as follows: angelic aromas are subtle and reassuring; spirit-guide scents may be much more powerful, and spark strong emotions associated with the person who has passed. If this happens to you, allow the experience to unfold and accept what is being shown to you through this scent. Thank your guides, then ask your angels to step forward so you can continue your connection with them.

ANGELIC SCENTS

You can choose specific essential oils to connect with a particular angel (see below). Sandalwood and frankincense as incense or essential oil have long been used in spiritual practice to aid prayer, meditation, and a connection with the divine; frankincense was also one of the gifts of the Magi in the Bible. If you like these aromas, add a few drops of the essential oils to the water bowl of an aromatherapy burner, or burn some incense on your angel altar (see Tip 18). There are many more aromatherapeutic associations with archangels, but here is a selection using the most commonly available oils:

- **Haniel** Geranium, rose, ylang-ylang, lemon, jasmine
- **Raphael** Lavender,* bergamot, geranium, chamomile, juniper, sandalwood, pine
- **Michael** Basil, clary sage, sandalwood
- **Zadkiel** Lavender,* rosemary,* frankincense, sandalwood, peppermint, spearmint
- **Jophiel** Lemon, bergamot, jasmine
- **Gabriel** Neroli, clary sage, melissa

Avoid handling during pregnancy

27 How to Make Your Own Angel Mist

An Angel Mist is a solution of water and essential oils, blessed with the healing energy of your angels. It's sprayed around your aura, or energy field, to lift your personal vibration, to clear away negative energy, and to prepare a space for angelic communication.

With your angels' help, you can dedicate your Angel Mist to any good purpose: love, abundance, courage, focus, or confidence, for example. You can also choose an essential oil for its specific benefits (see the list on page 84), but always go with an aroma you love. A gorgeous fragrance heightens your senses, bringing you closer to the vibrational level of the angelic realm.

You will need still spring water, ideally, but if you don't have any to hand, you can use distilled water (ironing water) or take water straight from the faucet.

* Fill a mister bottle with about 1 fl. oz (30ml) water and place it on a table. Now add one or two drops of an essential oil of your choice, or choose from the list on page 84.

* Gently inhale the scent. Call upon your angels—you can visualize meeting them on a pathway strewn with beautiful flower petals and herbs. Feel the subtle shift in energy when your angels connect and come closer.

* Hold the bottle in your right hand and attune the spring water by asking your angels to bless it: "My Angels, please bless this essence." Then speak aloud what you would like your Angel Mist to do. When you are ready, thank your angels.

* Gently shake the bottle, and it is ready to use. Store your Angel Mist for up to three months in a cool place away from sunlight and heat, to preserve its energy. You can mist your home (see Tip 28) and your aura, as below.

HAVE AN AURA SHOWER

You aura holds information about your beliefs, which can manifest in your physical body for good or ill. Regularly spraying your aura with Angel Mist helps to cleanse and release any negativity before it manifests; it also helps you "rebalance" after feeling stressed or overwhelmed. If you are a healer, misting your aura helps protect you before a session and cleanse afterward, so your client's emotions do not linger around you or the healing room.

* Hold the bottle above your head and spray twice over the top of your head, about 6 inches (15 cm) from your crown, letting the droplets descend like a shower. Stand still for a few moments, inhaling the soft scent, the fine touch of the mist, and your angels all around you.

OILS AND THEIR MEANINGS

Essential oils have many therapeutic attributes. Here is a selection:

- **Angelica root:** Healing, awareness of angels
- **Bergamot:** Balancing, uplifting, helps low mood
- **Chamomile:** Healing, calming
- **Clary sage:** Dreams and inspiration
- **Eucalyptus:** Clear-thinking, purifying
- **Frankincense:** Divine connection, meditation, protection
- **Geranium:** Energy, love, fertility, balance
- **Jasmine:** Sensuality, joy
- **Lavender*:** Calming, balancing, healing, love, peace, purification
- **Lemon:** Joy and laughter, vitality
- **Melissa:** Calming, meditation, compassion
- **Neroli:** Balance, creativity, meditation
- **Peppermint*:** Money, prosperity, clarity, intuition
- **Pine:** Cleansing, healing
- **Rose:** Love, compassion
- **Rosemary*:** Focus, memory, purification
- **Sage*:** Cleansing, wisdom
- **Sandalwood:** Calm, protection, spirituality
- **Spearmint*:** Money, prosperity, protection
- **Ylang-ylang:** Love, peace, beauty

Please note that some essential oils have contraindications and should not be used during pregnancy. Check with the vendor when you buy them, and buy from a reputable supplier.

Angel Mist Recipes

PROTECTION MIST

3 drops lavender* essential oil

3 drops frankincense essential oil

2 drops sage* essential oil

Mantra to say as you spray:

"I am protected and safe."

ABUNDANCE MIST

3 drops lavender* essential oil

2 drops peppermint* essential oil

3 drops spearmint* essential oil

Mantra to say as you spray:

"I am a happy, healthy, successful person."

LOVE MIST

3 drops lavender* essential oil

3 drops rose absolute** or geranium essential oil

2 drops rosemary* essential oil

Mantra to say as you spray:

"I am loved and happy."

DE-STRESS MIST

3 drops lavender* essential oil

2 drops sandalwood essential oil

3 drops geranium essential oil

Mantra to say as you spray:

"I am relaxed and calm."

*Avoid during pregnancy

**Rose absolute is an expensive oil to buy, so if you prefer, substitute with geranium.

28 Cleanse Your Space with the House Angel

Whenever you need to shift the energy in your home, call upon angel Taharial. He is the angel of the house, sending you domestic wings—you can call upon him when you need to do speedy housework. More importantly, he is also the angel of purification. He helps you space-cleanse, lifting your home's vibration.

Our homes carry the energy of our experiences and emotions. They hold an energetic record of all the events of the home, and when these memories are not cleared out, the atmosphere can become dull, heavy, and distracting; it can become hard to feel settled and get things done. Your home may be holding predecessor energy—the energy imprint left by previous occupants, which may go back years and years. Having a "clear" space in which to live and maybe work means you can be more open to connecting with the higher realms. When your home is free from clutter (whether physical or spiritual), it's easier to welcome in your angels.

Before you try any of the cleansing rituals here, it's important to connect with the soul of your home. There may be things you need to understand about your house before you begin the cleansing rituals. If you have tried cleansing your space before but don't feel that much has changed, it could be because there is an unaddressed issue.

TALK TO THE SOUL OF YOUR HOME

Find what feels like the center of your living room. Light a candle or some incense and sit quietly. It's best if you are alone in the house, or at least alone in the communal parts—in that no one else is in the family rooms, dining rooms, and kitchen—so that you're not distracted.

* Ground, protect yourself, and open up before you begin (see pages 9–10). When you sense the vibrations of your angels, listen intently to your inner voice to make a connection with the voice of the home. When you sense a presence, ask a question to yourself or quietly aloud. You might hear the house talk back.

* Now ask the house what happened before you were there or why things in your house keep moving around or breaking. If you sense an answer, ask the house if you've understood correctly. A tingling feeling or shift in temperature will tell you that your connection is strong, and confirms that you have understood.

* Call upon angel Taharial and ask that what has happened in the past be cleansed. If you need to reassure your house that you will care for it (some houses feel neglected), just say so. Thank angel Taharial and the soul of your home, and blow out the candle.

* Thank your angels, and close down (see page 11).

SPACE-CLEARING WITH ANGEL MIST

* Take a spritzer bottle and fill it half-full with water. Add two drops of lavender* essential oil and two drops of sage* essential oil to about 1 fl. oz (30ml) spring water, distilled water, or tap water. Lavender oil helps return the energy of a space to neutral, while sage is for cleansing and protection. This is optional, but if you have a small selenite or rutilated quartz crystal, place it in the bottle. Selenite connects you with your

Energy-Sensing

If the energy in a room or home feels very low, such as when a place has been empty for a long time, you might like to begin by "energy-sensing" before you mist. This helps you to tune into problem areas and focus on releasing any energy blocks. To do this, ask your angels to show you where you need to cleanse the most. You can visualize this by sensing your angel standing behind you, guiding you; your third eye chakra (the one between your eyebrows) turns into a search beam. See this as indigo light radiating from your third eye, projecting right across the rooms as you walk through it, sensing any areas that feel stuck or blocked. Use your senses like a radar, really feeling the vibration of the space. With practice, you will do this quickly and with ease. Some people may "scan" buildings naturally, and pick up not just on low energy but also on spirits who inhabit the building.

Active spirits in a place are usually people who lived in that building or had a strong attachment to it. They may show you part of their life experience when you are in "their" space. You may sense their presence as a perfume or an unpleasant smell, a color, or even a vague form at the corner of your eye, in your peripheral vision. They might move objects around or interfere with electrical items or water, turning faucets on and off.

As a sensitive person, always ground and protect yourself before entering a building that may have spirit presence, and certainly before cleansing your own space. You can carry with you a stone for protection, such as black obsidian, black tourmaline, or hematite.

If you encounter a spirit presence, send them light. Ask your angels to bless and heal that spirit so they may find peace.

third eye chakra, activating your intuition, while rutilated quartz draws off negative energy and gives protection. Alternatively, you can use a small piece of clear quartz crystal, which will magnify the effect of the essential oils.

* Tune in to Taharial, the house angel, and ask for help in cleansing the atmosphere with the mist. Hold the bottle in your right hand and see your angel pouring light into the bottle and activating it.

* Thank your angel, then ritually walk around your room, spraying in all the corners, and wherever you feel that the energy is heavy or dense. Open the windows and play some of your favorite uplifting music—this lifts the vibration and helps the energy to shift.

Store your cleansing mist for up to three months in a cool place away from sunlight or heat, to preserve its energies.

You might also like to boost the vibration after you have cleansed with Angel Mists for love, protection, de-stressing, or abundance (see Tip 27).

* *Please note that lavender and sage oils are to be avoided during pregnancy.*

When to Cleanse

- After an argument
- After illness
- If you would like more visitors (as the energy in your home may be dull and uninviting)
- After a party
- After a major decision
- When you feel tired
- When you have moved into a new home
- Before you move house

Cleansing with Salt, Incense, or Smudge Sticks

Instead of using mist to cleanse, sprinkle some salt in the four corners of the rooms you want to purify (use whatever salt you have—table salt is fine). This is a great ritual for banishing all kinds of negative vibes.

* Ground, protect, and open up (see pages 9–10). Call upon Taharial, the House Angel, to help you release this old energy and purify your home as you sprinkle the salt crystals. Thank this angel, close down (see page 11), and leave the salt to do its work for as long as you feel is right.

* If you use incense, sage incense is a great cleanser. You can also use a smudge stick (a bundle of herbs, usually comprising sage and/or meadowsweet, for cleansing sacred spaces. You can make your own using dried sage leaves and dried lavender and/or rosemary). Walk around your home with the lit incense or smudge stick and call upon Taharial, as above. Take a small saucer with you to catch the embers. Extinguish the incense or smudge stick when you are finished, and close down (see page 11).

29 Ask your Angels to Help You Find Lost Things

Archangel Chamuel is known for helping you find things that are lost. He understands how items can seem to disappear, and he also wants to help you put things in the right place. He will help you find anything, from your keys to your direction and purpose in life. As an angel of justice, he wants things to go right for you. You can also call upon Rochel, the angel of lost objects.

A friend was always losing her glasses (and the more stressed she was at work, the more often she misplaced them). Thankfully, her colleagues knew her of old and were used to finding them in the restroom, by the kettle, or abandoned in meeting rooms, and she always had them returned to her. Although she couldn't break the habit of a lifetime and become a person who didn't lose things, she believed her glasses were always returned to her because she kept a tiny carved crystal angel, wrapped in a piece of cotton, secreted in her glasses case. While she couldn't always remember where she had left her glasses, she had asked her angels to help her, and they regularly did—through other people.

If you really think you've lost something for good, you can dowse to get more information as to its whereabouts.

HOW TO DOWSE WITH YOUR ANGELS

To dowse you need something that will act as a pendulum, i.e. a weight on a chain or string. Ideally, work with a crystal pendulum, or use a pendant necklace (avoid magnetic stones such as hematite, though, as this can skew your reading). Alternatively, make your own pendulum with a ring on a chain or piece of string.

* Ground, protect, and open up to your angels (see pages 9–10).
* Now tune in to your pendulum. Close your eyes and hold your pendulum for a few moments. Feel its energy. You might find your palms becoming hotter or colder as you do this. Open your eyes, take your pendulum in your dominant hand, and rest your elbow somewhere comfortable so the pendulum chain can move freely and your hand and elbow are stable. Now ask your pendulum an obvious question, such as "Is my name xx?" Wait and you will see the

pendulum begin to move without any input from you. It may move in a circular motion, clockwise, or anticlockwise; it may move backward and forward in a line. Now ask another "yes" question. This should confirm the movement your pendulum makes for "yes." Do the same for "no." If the pendulum doesn't move, or if it is static and trembles, this may not be the right time to dowse; wait one day and try again, or rephrase your question.

* Call upon Archangel Chamuel to help you find your lost items. Wait for him to come close, and sense his presence through the signs you know— maybe a tingling, a color you sense in your mind's eye, a feeling of warmth and love, or perhaps an aroma.

* Walk around your home or office room by room and observe if your pendulum moves into the "yes" or "no" position. The stronger the energy of your "yes," the closer you are to your lost item. Keep moving around to sense the strongest energy, then search close to where you are standing. If the pendulum doesn't move, try one more time, rephrasing the question, but if nothing happens then, it's likely the item is not in this place or cannot be found. Thank your angels whether you find your item or not. Not every lost object can be located, and your angels will let you know either way.

* If you don't wish to dowse, simply ask for a sign about the whereabouts of your item, saying:

"Archangel Chamuel, please help me find xx." Thank your angels, and close down (see page 11).

* Let go of the outcome. Trust that your angels will find a way to help you remember where your item is—this can happen through someone you know reminding you, or a stranger, like an Earth Angel, helping you (see Tip 23). It's important to add immediacy to your request, as time is not a consideration for angels unless you ask for it. For example, say: "Please help me find my item as soon as you are able. Thank you." We can only keep looking for something for so long before declaring it officially lost, so decide how long this is; a moon cycle of 28 days may be enough. In the meantime, have faith that your angels will be guiding you.

30 *Asking Angels for "Happy" Money*

It's okay to ask your angels to help you with money. The best way to phrase this, though, is to ask your angels to bring you "happy" money, or simply "happiness." If more money will truly bring you happiness at this moment, your angels will help you.

If having money won't ultimately solve a problem and make you happy, asking for it won't help. The key is attuning to a prosperous mindset, when you believe you can have whatever you need and that your angels and the universe will always provide for and protect you. When you truly feel this, no matter how depleted your finances, you're on the prosperity path, because you've already raised your vibration. And the higher your vibration (see page 76), the more things become possible because you attract higher-level beings, friends, influences— and more of everything. This is the place from which to ask your angels for happiness and "happy money."

MAKING A MONEY ANGEL

Making a money angel and keeping it in your wallet shows you believe and trust that angels will help you become happy and prosperous. You can buy a crystal angel or make one by cutting a small angel shape or some wings out of a piece of paper or card. Keep the crystal angel in the zipped coin section of your wallet, and your paper angel where you keep any photos.

* Before your money angel can get to work, you will need to give it this blessing. First, ground, protect, and open up to your angels (see pages 9–10). Hold your money angel in your palms and close your eyes. Ask your angels to come close so that you feel their energy, and then name your money angel, saying three times: "I name you my money angel. Help me be prosperous and happy." Thank your angels and your new money angel.

THE QUICK MONEY-POT MANTRA

This is a mantra you can chant every day to keep money flowing. Don't wait until you are desperate for money before you ask for help; ask when you are feeling really up—when your personal vibration is high and joyful. Asking from a place of happiness helps you attract more of the same, more easily, because you're in the flow. It takes a lot more energy to get into a positive mindset for money magic when you are in a negative place in yourself. If you are feeling low and depleted, ask your angels to help raise your vibration before trying this brilliant mantra. It is used by Jayne, who runs the successful spiritual business Psychic Sisters—her angels and this mantra keep money rolling in.

You will need your favorite angel figurine, or the small money angel you keep in your wallet (see above).

* Perform this mantra morning and night. Ground, protect, and open up (see pages 9–10). Now connect with your angel by holding the figurine in your hand and waiting until you feel your angel near. Say: "I am a money pot" quickly ten times, running them together, so you are making a mantra:

Iamamoneypot, Iamamoneypot, Iamamoneypot

See the money pot in your mind's eye as you speak, and generate a feeling of excitement as the pot glows with overflowing gold. Attach your good feelings to the image as you recite the words, and know that, with your angel's help too, money will soon be coming to you. Say thank you to your angels. You deserve your angels' help.

You may find that you get your money in an indirect way, through an Earth Angel (see Tip 23), a flash of inspiration, guidance through numbers (see Tip 2), or becoming aware of a talent you can use to support yourself and others.

31 How to Connect with the Angels of Your Garden

Angel Sachluph is the angel of plants and flowers, and Angel Cathetel is the angel of the garden. These nature-protecting angels will help your garden grow.

Place an image of an angel in your garden—such as an angel-shaped mirror or piece of stained glass, a stone or crystal figure in a container, a stone cherub, or angel wings, or you could plant a seedling or buy a plant that appeals to you. Cathetel's plant is lavender, but you can choose any plant that evokes your guardian angel or other angels, too.

You might call the angels into your garden with color, with spring bluebells for Archangel Michael, cerise roses for love and Archangel Haniel, lilies and orange gerberas for Archangel Gabriel, but always go with whichever plants and flowers you adore the most. Painting angel wings on flat stones and finishing them with exterior varnish adds an angelic touch to even the tiniest of outdoor spaces.

MAKING AN ANGEL MEMORY GARDEN

Acknowledging other people's positive role in your life is a pathway to self-healing if you are dealing with loss. Making a memory garden means you can create something small but beautiful in the name of a beloved person or pet.

Angel statues have in recent years become shrines for bereaved parents; "Angels of Hope" are placed in parks where the bereaved can gather and pray together for their lost children.

You will need an angel figurine to watch over your memory garden. You can use figurines of butterflies or birds, too. Buy a pot of rosemary for remembrance, a pot of sage, for healing sorrow, and one more—choose from borage with its pretty blue leaves for joy and courage, lavender for calm, or common (garden) angelica, with its white flower clusters, for spiritual protection. Three is an important number in this ritual because it is dynamic—a number of creation that keeps memory alive in a positive way, so you can move forward while never forgetting the person's role in your life.

* Make an angel blessing scroll (see Tip 21) naming the person or pet. If you have space in your garden, plant the herbs and bury the scroll close to the rosemary. If you are making your memory garden on a windowsill, balcony, or terrace, keep the herbs in their pots.

* Hold your angel figurine for a few moments. Beginning by grounding, protecting, and opening up (see pages 9–10), and naming the person or pet. Say: "Angel Zadkiel, please bless the memory of [name]. I dedicate this space to xx. May s/he rest in peace in my heart and my memory. I give thanks for the love [or inspiration/joy/other quality] they have given me." Thank Archangel Zadkiel. Place the angel figurine by the herbs, and close down (see page 11).

* Tend your memory garden regularly and know that your angels are caring for your loved ones.

32 Talk to Your Angels with Candles

Lighting a candle signals a change in energy and mood. Candles have been used ritually for thousands of years to signify the shift from one state of being to another, from this world to the world of spirit and the realm of the angels. Lighting a candle is a way to gently prepare a space for spiritual work. It creates an ambience of calm and readiness for angel communication.

Whenever you feel you cannot set aside time to meditate with your angels, simply light a candle on your angel altar while you are in the same room doing other tasks. This symbolizes your desire to have your angels in your life, and nourishes your connection.

There are also particular candles associated with angels and archangels. So if you want to ask Archangel Raphael to help you with healing, for example, buy a green candle. Green is Raphael's color, and the color of healing and the heart chakra (see Tip 12). You can anoint the candle with one of Raphael's essential oils, bergamot (for other archangels and their essential oils, see Tip 26). To do this, tip a few drops of essential oil onto the tip of the unlit candle, near the wick, and gently rub it over the surface of the candle (use a square of kitchen roll to do this, rather than touching the oils directly, as some are skin irritants). Place the candle in a holder. Light the candle, close your eyes, and focus on your breath.

* Ground, protect, and open up to your angels (see pages 9–10). Ask Raphael to help you by addressing him by name, stating your wish; feel his presence and angelic love. Say thank you, and put your trust in him. Let go of any anxiety or worry, and believe that Raphael hears your wish and will do everything he can to help you. When you have finished, leave the candle burning for a minute or two until your feel you are fully back in the room, then extinguish it. If you have asked your angel for help, see your wish as the candle smoke drifting up to the universe. Close down (page 11).

You can place the candle on your angel altar to empower your request. If you don't have the color of candle you need, don't worry. The candle color empowers the ritual but doesn't exclude you from communicating with your chosen angel(s). Just take a plain white or yellow candle and visualize your chosen angel's color as you light it. Your belief and intention to communicate are what counts. Just light a candle, and begin.

Archangels and Candle Colors

- **Raphael** Green
- **Gabriel** Orange
- **Michael** Blue
- **Haniel** Pink, turquoise

- **Uriel** Red
- **Zadkiel** Violet
- **Jophiel** Yellow
- **Raziel** Indigo

- **Metatron** White
- **Auriel** Silver

33 How to Meet Your Angels in the Bath

Sounds strange? This is one of the lesser-known yet most magical rituals to bring you closer to the angelic realms and your spirit guides. Spirit guides are generally believed to have lived on earth before, and, like your angels, dedicate themselves to guiding you through your life experiences.

Meeting both your angels and your guides can be a profound experience, so take this ritual very gently.

* Run a bath, then add some natural salt to the water, for purity. Turn off the lights in the bathroom and, if it's not too cold outdoors, open the bathroom window a little. Let your eyes adjust to the darkness.

* Before you get into the bath, ground, protect, and open up to your angels (see pages 9–10).
* Get into the tub and relax for at least five minutes. Sense your angels coming closer to you.
* Now pull out the plug of the bathtub, but don't get out. Lie back again and feel the drag of the water against your skin as the level drops. At this stage, you might feel slightly absurd—and the water may be gushing noisily away—but stay lying back. When there are just a few inches of water left, you will feel the incredible weight of your body and a surge of well-being, as if you are entering a dreamlike state. Now begin your own visualization, or try this: see yourself walking down a pathway, alongside a river. Notice all the sensations of the grass underfoot, the birds you meet, the crunch of your footsteps on the path. Then find a place to sit. You are feeling more deeply relaxed than ever. What or whom do you meet?
* Stay in the tub until all the water has drained away. Carefully get out of the bath when you are ready, and close down your connection (see page 11).

34 When You are Ill your Guardian Angel will Hold Your Hand

*Your guardian angel will come close while you are ill; you just have to ask.
If you try this meditation at bedtime, ask Archangel Michael to ground the
healing and close down for you in advance if you fall asleep partway through.*

* First, do the grounding, protection, and opening-up visualization (see pages 9–10). Gently speak the name of your guardian angel aloud or silently, or just say: "My Angel, please join me now. Thank you." Breathe in and sense your body filling with your guardian angel's light.

* Ask your guardian angel to bring Raphael, the healing archangel. Imagine his color, emerald-green, pouring into every cell of your body. Sense his wings around you, giving you an angel hug. Connect with this feeling of calm and protection. Now ask for what you need. This might be help with pain in a part of your body, help dealing with tiredness and exhaustion, or perhaps the patience to rest and care for yourself.

* Trust your senses. If you have any pain or discomfort, the quality of the pain may start to feel different. Trust this feeling and stay with it. Imprint the feeling of protection and healing as a way to show your body how to heal itself. The angels see you as a perfect being. See yourself as perfect, as they do, and begin to generate a vibration of wellness.

* Watch your thoughts. Your words have an energy imprint—negative words can put you in a place of victimhood. Try to connect with a true sense of wellness, perhaps by visualizing words such as "relaxed," "vital," or "at home with myself."

* Listen to your body, don't fight it. Fighting pain and discomfort takes energy. Pain is a message from your body—what is your body trying to tell you? Send compassion to the parts that hurt.

* Place your left hand on your higher heart chakra and your right hand on your solar plexus (see the illustration on the following page). This connects you with love and energy—at a spiritual level, your angels' universal love and your soul wisdom. Your body and mind know how to be well. Sense Raphael's healing light flowing through your arms and palms into these chakras. Rest and let the energy flow. You can do this chakra self-healing exercise every day to support your health, even when you are well.

Chakra self-healing

* Ask Archangel Michael to ground the healing in this lifetime, and any other lifetimes you had before.
* Close down when you feel ready (see page 11).

AN ANGEL SYMBOL AT YOUR BEDSIDE HELPS YOU SLEEP

For healing sleep, you can place any of these items on your bedside table or nightstand. They are symbols of protection and your angels, who watch over you. If you don't have any of the crystals as individual stones, look through your jewelry collection to see if you have that crystal as a necklace, earrings, or bracelet, and place that by your bed instead.

* Your angel crystal (see Tip 6)
* Lapis lazuli, for protection, good sleep, dreams, and spiritual connection
* Hematite, for grounding and protection. Also helps insomnia
* Celestite, the stone of heaven. Helps you remember your dreams
* A figurine of Raphael, the healing angel
* Any other angel figurine you love
* Charms: Feathers, wings, angel forms
* If you have children who are suffering from nightmares, the crystal chrysoprase, a heart chakra stone, helps protect them from bad dreams. Place it on their bedside table, or they can sleep with it under their pillow (of course,

this isn't suitable for younger children, who may mistake it for a sweet!). You can also try lepidolite, which is calming and balancing, brings emotional healing, and protects against negativity.

Now dedicate the items to deep, restful sleep, as follows.

* First ground, protect, and open up (see pages 9–10). Set your intention to have a great night's sleep and generate how you want to feel tomorrow morning. Take yourself back to the last time you felt this way and reconnect with that feeling of contentment. (If you are dedicating crystals for your children, visualize them sleeping well and waking feeling happy and relaxed.)

* Place the items in your right hand (if you have lots of objects, you'll need to do this more than once, depending on what can fit in your palm). Attune to each object for a few minutes by holding it and feeling its vibration, then call in your guardian angel.

* Ask your guardian angel to bless the objects, by saying: "My Angel, please bless these objects [and name them in turn] and watch over me." Sense your angel's white light passing through your crown, third eye, throat, and heart chakras, then down your left arm to your palm and to the object/s you're holding. Really feel the angelic vibration in your body as you make the

Crystals and Cell Phones

Cell phones emit an electromagnetic field, and some people sense that this affects them in a negative way. If you are highly sensitive to energy, you may need to protect yourself from cell-phone emanations. Many of us have our phones switched on at night because we need them for an alarm. Ideally you would switch back to a non-electrical clock, but if this isn't convenient for you, crystals can help. Try amazonite, black tourmaline, and sodalite to absorb cell-phone emanations. Place them between you and your phone on your bedside table or nightstand.

connection between your guardian angel, you, and the objects. Now ask your angel to bring you restful sleep, and to watch over you. Thank your guardian angel, and close down (see page 11).

35 Connect with Your Angels Through Flowers

Angels love flowers. Flowers are highly sensitive to energy and resonate with the angelic realm. Make it a ritual to offer fresh, pretty flowers to your angels whenever you can afford to. Choose blooms that are bright and beautiful.

Certain flowers are dear to angels. You can display them on your angel altar, or find a greetings card or flower photo you have taken and frame it. Or, grow them in a special part of your garden dedicated to your angel practice (see Tip 31). Here is a selection of flowers and their associations:

- **Gardenia:** Joy and abundance; prosperity
- **Honeysuckle:** Love; ability to listen
- **Rose:** Love and passion
- **Iris:** The divine messenger of God; represents the Annunciation
- **Violet:** Simplicity
- **White lily:** Peace. Archangel Gabriel has been depicted holding a fleur de lys, or three-petaled lily, when visiting Mary for the Annunciation of her child. The three petals stand for the Holy Trinity
- **Snowdrop:** Hope. This flower was given to Eve by an angel who turned a snowflake into a snowdrop to reassure her that her misery would not last.

MAKING A FLOWER ESSENCE

Flowers have a unique vibration, or energy "signature." The vibration of a flower can be transferred into water to make a flower essence. Sprayed from a mister bottle, a flower essence can banish negative energy and raise your vibration, helping you connect with the angelic realms.

To make an essence, parts of a flower are bathed in spring water and left in sunlight or moonlight for hours or days until the energies are imprinted in the water. These essences are different from essential oils (see Tip 26), which are the distilled concentrate of aromatic plants; flower essences are infusions of flowers in water—they are very gentle, diluted preparations that work on the mind and emotions. Some popular flower essence brands are Bach Flower Remedies, Vie de la Rose, and Australian Bush Flower Essences. You can also make your own flower essence, as follows.

ANGEL ROSE RECIPE

* Take some fallen rose petals. Float them in a large bowl of spring water or tap water, and place the bowl on a windowsill or in a sunny spot outside. Let the sunlight play on the petals for up to three hours. Then discard the petals and decant the flower essence into a mister bottle.

* Dedicate the flower essence to your work with angels by calling your angels to you and asking them to bless the flower essence (see Tip 26).
* When you have finished, thank your angels, and close down (see page 11).

You can spray your aura before your angel rituals (spray twice over the crown of your head, about 6 in./15 cm above it), and spray around your angel altar and elsewhere in your home to keep the atmosphere gentle and harmonious.

Keep your essence bottle in a cool place away from sunlight and heat to protect its energy.
(Do not ingest the essence.) It will keep for up to seven days.

36 Angels and the "New" Chakras

The more you work with your angels, and the more we raise our collective consciousness, the more likely it is that your multidimensional chakras are awakening.

As we develop spiritually, we as humanity are going through a process known as ascension—when our consciousness expands and we become more spiritually aware. As we "shift," new energies become available to us, in the form of "new" or developing chakras. As our awareness expands and our spirits call out for higher knowledge, these energy vortices are opening up to meet our needs. These "new" chakras reflect our growing vibration and higher consciousness as we enter the fifth dimension—the realm of light.

The chakras listed below are assisting us on our journey:

- **STELLAR GATEWAY:** Connection point to the cosmos, which opens as humanity spiritually awakens
- **SOUL STAR:** Karma and soul wisdom
- **FOURTH EYE CHAKRA:** Spiritual direction-giver; connection to the higher self
- **ALTA MAJOR CHAKRA:** Past lives, expanding consciousness, divine plan
- **HIGHER HEART, OR THYMUS CHAKRA:** Universal love; the "seat of the soul"

- **HEART SEED CHAKRA:** Soul memory
- **HARA/NAVEL CHAKRA:** Life purpose; also the emotional aspect of the sacral chakra
- **EARTH STAR:** Grounding and connection

Your angels may be already helping you "upgrade," awakening your higher chakras so that the flow of communication speeds up. It's like installing a more powerful optical cable, which can transmit higher-frequency messages.

Here's what Diane, an angel intuitive, has to say about her "upgrade" experiences:

"I know my guides and angels are taking me to the next level when I suddenly start craving high-frequency foods—fruit, vegetables, juices, smoothies, usually for a few weeks (or months, when it's a big upgrade). It's like a period of preparation. I also start drinking lots of water, which I suddenly feel guided to bless. Then, sure enough, within a few weeks, the words start coming in, long passages of text just float into my mind while I'm doing the washing up or as I'm waking up in the morning, and the communication with my guides and angels becomes clearer than ever.

Stellar Gateway

Soul Star

Fourth Eye (at the back and above the head)

(Crown)

Angelic
(Third Eye)

(Throat)

Higher Heart

(Heart)

Heart Seed

(Solar Plexus)

Hara

(Sacral)

(Base)

For exact chakra positions, see the
"Developing Chakras" listing on
page 109.

Earth star

"I feel myself being guided so strongly in almost every area of life. My crown feels lit up and the angels start speaking to me constantly in signs, numbers, songs, and phrases. It's as if all of this potential has always been there, but it suddenly intensifies dramatically.

"I often wake up knowing I've been to other dimensions to study, or traveling around giving healing or teaching, and waking up feeling exhausted is something I've had to get used to. I've found that by working with my "fifth dimension" team, I can find solutions to most of the disruptions caused by the upgrades. For example, I know how to energetically fill myself up in the morning so I can still do my work, even when I wake up exhausted. I also find that when the inspiration is coming thick and fast, I need to meditate more so I can ground myself and keep my energy clear enough to allow the process to flow.

"Sometimes new guides start to appear, bringing more ideas or lifting the work into their higher frequency, and despite any temporary intensity, any disruption that comes from connecting with these beautiful beings is always outweighed by bliss."

Are you upgrading?

What to look out for:

* Intense dreams or feeling exhausted when you wake. You might already know that your angels are trying to give you more information, and it is common to feel that this is happening at night while you are sleeping. You might wake feeling as though you've just run a mental marathon. If so, your angels are sending you to night school!
* Changing your eating habits for the better and drinking more water
* A stronger sense of guidance
* Ringing in one or both ears. This can be auric transmission, a sign of high-frequency communication. If it is too loud, do ask your angels to turn down the sound
* If you are already a healer, finding that the angels are showing you new techniques during your practice

37 Awakening the Higher Heart Chakra—Universal Love

The higher heart or thymus chakra is located between the throat and the heart chakras. The higher heart chakra activates as we become more heart-centered and "connected" in our way of living; it is the chakra of universal love.

When we work with the heart chakra (love at a personal level) and the higher heart chakra (universal love), we create a gateway for spiritual ascension. In practice, this means that your thoughts, feelings, and deeds become directed by the wisdom of your heart. Your compassion for strangers grows. You feel more connected with the earth, with others, and with the "true you." You may sense what your purpose is in this lifetime.

This meditation connects you with your higher heart and opens up the pathway to universal love.

* Begin with the grounding, protection, and opening-up ritual (see pages 9–10), and sit comfortably.
* Sense your angels' loving vibration as you connect with them. Feel their wings enclosing you; you are safe and loved.
* Place your hand on the higher–heart chakra, between your heart and throat chakras (see illustration on page 105). Feel the growing heat in your hand as you welcome in your angels and universal love. Feel the warmth as a channel of pink light, flowing up from your heart, higher heart, throat, third eye, and crown chakras, and up to the angelic realms.
* Do you feel your heart and chest opening and relaxing? You might sense a change in your throat chakra, too. A feeling of intense love and deep peace—perhaps you might even notice a change in the rhythm of your heartbeat. Tune in with your senses.
* If you have your angel crystal (see Tip 6) or a rose quartz, you might like to hold it to your higher–heart chakra for a few moments. This imprints the crystal with this love vibration. Crystals have memories, and after this meditation you will be able to hold this crystal to reconnect with the feeling of universal love.

When you are ready, close down (see page 11). Don't worry if you don't get any of these responses the first time you practice this exercise. Your higher heart can gently awaken as you become ready.

Our Developing Chakras

STELLAR GATEWAY	12 in. (30 cm) above top of head	Archangels Metatron and Seraphina
SOUL STAR	6 in. (15 cm) above the crown	Archangels Zadkiel and Muriel
FOURTH-EYE CHAKRA	About 4 in. (10 cm) back from the crown chakra, just above the head	Archangel Christiel
FIFTH-EYE, ANGELIC, OR SOMA CHAKRA	Center of head at hairline	Archangel Tzaphkiel
ALTA MAJOR CHAKRA:	Base of the skull/back of neck	
HIGHER-HEART, OR THYMUS CHAKRA	Over the thymus gland, between the heart and throat chakras	Archangel Haniel
HEART-SEED CHAKRA	Base of the breastbone	Archangel Chamuel
HARA/NAVEL CHAKRA	Just above the navel	Archangel Gabriel
EARTH STAR	12–18 in. (30–45 cm) below the feet	Archangel Sandalphon

To work on higher chakras—the stellar gateway, soul star, and higher crown—you will need to activate the earth-star chakra in order to be fully grounded during any meditation. Archangel Metatron rules the stellar gateway, and his twin flame, Sandalphon, rules the earth star chakra—between them they create divine balance. Practices such as Angelic Reiki can help open up these chakras, or you can consult a lightworker or crystal healer, if this feels right for you.

38 Discover Your Angelic Chakra

You can activate the angelic chakra on your forehead to accelerate your spiritual development and angelic connection. You can practice this technique at the start of each day to tune in to your angels.

* Go through the grounding, protection, and opening-up rituals (see pages 9–10).
* Making a triangle with your thumbs and index fingers together, rest your index fingers (the top of the triangle) on the angelic chakra, and your thumbs on the third-eye chakra. This connects the third-eye chakra with the fifth-eye or angelic chakra, linking intuition with the point of angelic connection. The triangle you are making creates a spiritual gateway over the fourth- eye chakra, for manifesting dreams into reality. (Delta, the fourth letter of the Greek alphabet, is a triangle. The word derives from the Phoenician letter "dalet," which means "door.")
* Press gently on these two chakra points as you meditate on your angels and communicate with them.
* You might also like to lie down and place a crystal on each of these chakra points. Choose amethyst for the third-eye chakra, and quartz, or one of the angel stones in Tip 6, on the angelic chakra. Clear quartz crystals magnify and transmit energy, so will help your connection.

You might like to try Lemurian Seed, a form of clear quartz; this crystal is known as the "lightworkers' stone."

39 Talk to Your Angels with Angel Cards

Angel cards are a brilliant way to invite angels into your life. Keep them on display in a bowl and choose one at random for a daily affirmation. Making your own cards charges them with your energy and makes a strong connection with your angels.

MAKING COLOR CARDS

Take some colored pencils or poster paint or, if you don't have these, some old magazines. Cut seven card shapes from sturdy cardboard—they can be any size or shape you like.

Choose shades of these colors:

Red, orange, yellow, green, pink, blue, indigo, violet

You can color in the whole of the card in a color or paint a "swipe" on each. If you're using magazines, cut out color swatches and stick them onto the card. Now attune your cards.

* Ground, protect, and open up (see pages 9–10).
* Hold the cards in your right hand and really feel your angels' presence through your senses. Ask your angels to bless the cards, saying: "My Angels, please bless these cards. May my readings be for the good of everyone." When you are ready, thank your angels.
* Hold each card to your heart in turn, feeling your angels' wings around you.
* Shuffle the cards and choose one.

Past   *Present*   *Future*

What color do you see? This is your angel's message for you today:

- **Red** is for security. You are being asked to look at your identity and how safe you feel. This may relate to your home and life direction.
- **Orange** is for sexuality and self-expression. What do you need to share and create?
- **Yellow** is good health, strength, and joy.
- **Rose-pink** is for love and compassion.
- **Green** denotes healing and protection.
- **Blue** is for speaking your truth and communicating clearly with others.
- **Indigo** is for intuition and psychic connection.
- **Violet** is for transformation and your spiritual path.

✳ Close down after the reading (see page 11).

GIVING AN ANGEL–CARD READING

You can use angel cards or your own color cards to do simple readings for yourself and your friends.

After grounding, protecting, and opening up to your angels (see pages 9–10), shuffle the cards to imprint your energy on them. If you are reading for a friend, ask them to shuffle the cards. Then fan out the cards on a table and choose three using your left hand (traditionally, the left hand is known as "the hand of fate"). The first card you pick represents the past, the second shows the present, and the third the future.

* Try explaining the card meanings as if you were telling a story. Your angels will help you interpret the cards further—sense any other images or words that come to you while you are reading the colors.
* When you have finished your reading, thank your angels and close down (see page 11).

MAKING MESSAGE CARDS

The channeled messages in the Directory (page 141) can be inspiration for your message cards, or you can make your own. Here's how:

* Go through the grounding and protection ritual (see pages 9–10).
* Take your angel journal (see Tip 19) or a notebook and pen. Connect with Archangel Metatron, the angelic scribe; ask him to come close, and thank him in advance for helping you.
* Take up your pen and sense your angel's energy around you, using all your senses. Now ask for a message. Write it down quickly and turn over the page. Do this again, for each message you receive, and repeat until you feel the energy shift. If you start to feel as though your mind is taking over and directing you, take a break, reconnect with your angels and/or Archangel Metatron, and continue.
* Cut out the words and place them in a small bowl on your angel altar.
* Thank your angels, and close down (see page 11).

Tip

If you're finding it difficult to trust a word you're getting—or if you're not getting anything—try this: hold your pen in your non-dominant hand (so if you are right-handed, hold the pen in your left hand, and vice versa). We use the non-dominant hand because it helps bypass your "thinking" mind, which can get in the way of your intuition. See what happens now.

40 Meet the Tarot Angels

Did you know that angels are part of the traditional tarot deck? You can work with tarot cards to connect with your angels and get messages quickly.

A traditional tarot deck of 78 cards has three cards that you can use for angel readings. Most contemporary tarot decks are interpretations of the Rider Waite Tarot (1910), and have angels on the Lovers, Temperance, and Judgment. These cards fall into the major arcana sequence of 22 "trump" cards, or major turning points:

- **VI THE LOVERS:** This is the card of Archangel Raphael. It means love and choices, showing a cherubim with bow and arrow and a man and woman. Some decks show the couple as Adam and Eve. The Marseilles deck (1701–15) depicts three people with the cherub, implying the need for a mature decision.
- **XIV TEMPERANCE:** The card of Archangel Michael, meaning reconciliation, negotiating, balancing; showing an angel pouring water between two vessels. Temperance is one of the four cardinal virtues, along with Justice, Strength, and Prudence.
- **XX JUDGMENT:** The card of Archangel Gabriel. It means a wake-up call; renewal, rebirth, assessing your life, a second chance; showing one or more angels blowing trumpets, echoing the Last Judgment from the Book of Revelation.

* First, ground, protect, and open up to your angels (see pages 9–10). Take your tarot deck and shuffle, imprinting your energy on the cards.
* Now take out the Lovers, Temperance, and Judgment. Place them face down on a table. Close your eyes and breathe deeply for a few minutes, until you feel calm and centered. Invite your angels to come closer to you. Open your eyes and choose one card. Turn it face up; this is your angel tarot card. Now see the card meaning from the list opposite.
* Close your eyes, hold the card loosely, and tune in, sensing the energy of your angels around you. Ask your angels to tell you more about what the card means in your life, and anything you might do. You might like to call in the Archangel of the card you have chosen. Feel the connection with your angels. If you sense a message from them, ask them: "Do you mean …?" Pay attention to all your senses—maybe feeling a slight tingling on your skin, cobwebs in your hair, or sensing colors, words, or images in your mind. This is your angels' way of giving you confirmation. They are telling you "Yes."

* When you are ready, thank your angels, open your eyes, and close down (see page 11).
You can place the card on your altar (see Tip 18) or carry it with you while you are traveling.

You can also try the past, present, and future reading using three cards (see Tip 39).

If you do tarot cards regularly, you will now know that when one of the angel cards comes up for you in a reading, it also tells you, along with its traditional meaning, that your angels are close by.

USING PLAYING CARDS

If you don't have tarot cards, take a deck of playing cards and find the Queen of Hearts, who is traditionally linked with angelic qualities. This is because her equivalent card in the tarot is the Queen of Cups, who stands for love, compassion, generosity, and relationships—the blessings of angels.

* Follow the ritual for tarot cards as above. After you have shuffled the cards, take out the Queen of Hearts and place her face up, then choose two other cards from your deck at random, face down, and place them either side of the Queen. Now turn both cards face up. Which suits do the cards come from?

- **SUIT OF CLUBS:** focus on ideas, inspiration
- **SUIT OF HEARTS:** focus on relationships
- **SUIT OF DIAMONDS:** focus on clear thinking
- **SUIT OF SPADES:** focus on money, home, and practicalities

* When you have finished your reading, close down (see page 11).

41 Angels and Cloud-Watching

Angels love nature, and they love you being in nature. They can "talk" to us in cloud formations—this way they can show themselves to lots of us at the same time.

A stunning pink Cloud Angel was seen over South Florida on March 13, 2013, the day the Vatican named Cardinal Jorge Mario Bergoglio as Francis I, the new Pope. A luminous figure with wings outstretched in a V shape appeared over Royal Palm Beach. Many witnesses took photographs of the angel, which had a halo and a bright channel of yellow-white light running down the center of its body. Many people who saw this Cloud Angel believed that the angels were celebrating the appointment of Pope Francis.

CONTEMPLATE ON A CLOUD

You might have a favorite place outdoors where you go to think and be with yourself: a riverside walk, a seat in your garden, or even a chair by a window from which you can gaze at the trees and the sky.

* Sit comfortably, and follow the grounding, protecting, and opening-up ritual (see pages 9–10).

* Close your eyes and begin to sense your angels' presence; are gently enfolding you with their wings. Really feel this with all your senses. Let your breathing relax; let your body stay relaxed as you feel your feet firmly grounded on the earth or floor.

Open your eyes gently, and gaze at the sky. Ask your angels to show you a sign. What do you see? Go beyond your vision and sense the cloud shapes and patterns, as if you can feel their texture. You might sense the shape of a feather or the wing of an angel. Perhaps there's a faint outline of a number (four means angels—see Tip 2). Maybe a feather shape drifts over the heavens.

THE ANGEL CLOUD IN ARIZONA

Tom Lumbrazo began seeing signs of angels several years after he nearly died in a car crash, but was saved by a voice telling him to slow down 30 seconds before the impact. After that time, Tom began to sense the signs of angels around him. One unforgettable morning, he had his first vision of an angel, which was shown to him again in the clouds as confirmation. He says: "I was in awe and excitement as I just could not believe what I saw. It was clearly an angel with a human face and body with huge wings that stretched over his head and down to nearly the ground. It was so detailed I could see each feather with the quality of an HD television picture. This angel appeared in two poses—one standing up with a sideways stance, and

the other on a horse, with him turning his head to look at me. I knew he wanted me to see him and to know that he was with me—but still I could not appreciate that this was a real angel.

"After that vision, I could not get those two images out of my head. The next day I felt called to go to Borders Books. I went to the metaphysical section and immediately saw a book on angels. I picked it up and turned to a page at random—and a chapter on Archangel Michael. The image of Michael in the book, showing him on his horse, was nearly exactly what I had seen in my vision. So at that moment, I knew I really did see an angel and specifically which one—Archangel Michael.

"This vision was proven a reality in May 2008 in a cloud my wife, Carol, and I saw in Sedona, Arizona. As we were walking an outdoor labyrinth at a church there, the clouds began to form over our heads, and as we finished walking the labyrinth, we looked up and there was the angel cloud: clearly, Archangel Michael on his horse. I immediately took several pictures of it, and one later became the cover photo for our first book, *Journey to the Clouds*.* Since that time, Archangel Michael has become woven into my everyday life; I receive messages from him on a daily basis. Now I know that he is always with me to assist me with my life and to guide me."
(* See page 144 for Tom's website, where you can see the picture.)

42 *Angels Love Music and Joyful Occasions*

Angels are attracted to happiness, and when you celebrate the wonderful things in life, know that your angels will always join you. They love to party too!

When you next attend a big event, a christening, or a graduation ceremony, you may see little signs of your angels around you. They might show you a feather, or you might feel them as a tingle in your arm or scalp. When two people join together at a wedding, both their guardian angels are present, rejoicing. Some people can see these angels manifesting during the wedding vows, and also see the auras or energy fields of the couple. The color pink in the couple's auras shows that their heart chakra energy is expanded and connected—they are in love.

WHEN ANGELS GIVE YOU MESSAGES THROUGH MUSIC

Playing music you love raises your personal vibration, bringing you closer to the angelic frequencies. But you don't have to play music intentionally to attract your angels. Angels can also give you messages in the words of the music you hear around you—on the radio, in the supermarket, or even in a track blasting from an iPod or phone on public transport.

Jayne knows that her father, who passed away some years ago, is with her when she hears Lionel Richie's "Dance With My Father" on the radio. She sees this as her angels letting her know that her dad is still around.

If a song stays in your head when you're away from the music, it's likely there's a message for you in the lyrics. And you might even loathe the song—if you do, listen to the words then say them to yourself as a phrase, or focus on the one word that is strongest, out of the context of the music.

Here's an example. Before visiting a client, Hayley, to give her Angelic Reiki healing, I (Liz) put the radio on for company while getting ready. While I was traveling to Hayley's home, one of the songs from the radio kept playing in my head. The Germans have a rather endearing name for this—*Ohrwurm*, or earworm. My earworm that morning was "Maria" sung by Debbie Harry. The words to the song include "Ave Maria," and that's what kept going around—Ave Maria. The second song I heard that wouldn't go away was "Annie's Song" by John Denver.

During the healing, the meaning of "Ave Maria" became clear, as the energy of the Ascended Master Mother Mary came to join us. Mary is known as the "Queen of the Angels" and her color is blue.

Although strongly part of the Catholic tradition, she is also seen as an Ascended Master and represents the principle of the divine feminine. Some of Hayley's health issues that came up during the healing centered on the sacral chakra, linked with creativity and reproduction. Mary had come during our healing session to bring healing and comfort; she is also renowned for healing the heart.

I then asked about "Annie's Song" too. "That's the favorite song of my sister and me," she replied. "I heard it just last night! This is our angel's way of saying we were tuned in."

Here's one more example. During an angel meditation weekend at a country hotel led by Jayne, the angels gave each member of her group the same song, at the same time.

It began when the angels showed Jayne a man in spirit who wanted to get a message to an elderly lady named Becka. Then Jayne heard a tune, "My Way" by Frank Sinatra. "What did your angels show you for this lady?" she asked her group, saying nothing about the song the angels had given her. "Music!" they chorused. "'My Way.'" Jayne's angels spoke to her again, saying how Becka's husband in spirit wanted her to sing the song for him. Becka was immediately sobbing—"My Way" had been their special song. "Can you sing it for him?" asked Jayne

gently. "I can't," croaked Becka tearfully. "I don't think I can do it." "That's okay, Becka," Jayne replied. Then they closed the meditation space for the day and wandered downstairs to relax and chat in the bar area of the hotel.

In the bar, a band was in rehearsal and the vocalist began to sing "My Way." Encouraged by the group, Becka got up with the others and together they sang the song for her late husband after all.

Tuning into the Angelic Frequency—528 Hertz

Recent research has led to an understanding that 528 Hz is the love frequency; it links the heart to heaven and our angels. This frequency cannot be found on a normally tuned piano or other instrument, which are tuned so that the A above middle C has a frequency of 440 Hz. The only way to produce 528 Hz exactly would be to use a synthesizer that allows you to set A to 444 Hz. This will make the C above middle C exactly 528 Hz.

The tone of 528 Hz has traditionally been used by healers and priests to generate transformations and miracles. The released version of John Lennon's song "Imagine" is in the key of C major, tuned to 528 Hz. You can find other examples of music tuned to 528 Hz on the internet.

Research by Dr. Joseph Puleo and Dr. Leonard Horowitz has helped us rediscover and understand the ancient Solfeggio tonal scale, comprising six notes, which were sung in Gregorian chants during church services.

THE "LOST" SOLFEGGIO SCALE

396 HZ: *liberating guilt and fear*

417 HZ: *undoing situations and making change*

528 HZ: *transformation and miracles; the repair frequency for damaged DNA*

639 HZ: *connection and understanding relationships*

741 HZ: *expression and solutions*

852 HZ: *awakening intuition*

43 Did Your Angels Grant Your Wish?

Sometimes, your request might not be granted because there is an issue with how you're doing the asking. To ask your angels for help and guidance, you need to connect with the right feeling. What's holding you back?

FEAR CONSCIOUSNESS/POVERTY CONSCIOUSNESS/VICTIMHOOD

Fear creates an energy block that gets in the way of communication with your angels. Fear of not getting your wish, of not having your needs met, or of not being good enough can block your messages to your angels. Desperation lowers your vibration so the angels can't hear you. The more negative and fearful your words and thinking patterns, the more likely it becomes that these thoughts can take form in the energy body. These "thought forms" can get in the way of manifesting, so look at your beliefs. Some of these beliefs about yourself may go very deep, and be buried in childhood experience. If so, it's time to work on letting these go.

If you ask your angels to help you with money, imagine now how you will feel when you have no money worries—to place yourself in the future as if the request has already been granted. Many people find this difficult, particularly if it's hard for them to remember a time and the feeling of financial stability. If this applies to you, ask your angels for help. With angels, you can ask for everything you need, so begin by asking for help with asking!

Practice a short meditation in which you invite your angels to join you, and help you feel positive about the outcome of your request. You could say,

"Please help me let go of fear/lack/uncertainty/anything in the way of manifesting."

Repeat your request to your angels, with feeling; thank them, and let go. It's also helpful to play music before you ask for help with asking. Music you love boosts your mood and your vibration (see Tip 42).

KEEPING YOUR PRAYERS PRIVATE

When you make requests to your angels, keep your prayers a secret. It's best not to share them with anyone else for now, because this dilutes the energy around your intention. This is a private matter between you and your angels. It's fine to share what happened with others after your wish has manifested, but best not before.

ARE YOU BEING DRAINED?

If you have negative, draining friends—who may of course still be lovely people, at heart—energize yourself in their company and send them love. They all have a role to play.

A very good friend of ours, Daphne, once reminded me of the saying: "Friends come into your life for a reason, a season, or a lifetime." Wise words indeed—"reason" and "season" friends are just as important as lifetime ones. The reasons and seasons are those people who seem to point you in the right direction and may literally change your life, but bow out when their work is done. They may even be Earth Angels, sent to intervene on behalf of the angels themselves (see Tip 23). From a spiritual perspective, negative friends are bringing you a lesson about yourself, helping you question your attitudes and values, and pointing you toward your higher purpose. They may be your reason or season friends.

Be kind to the negative people in your life. Treat them with compassion, and send them love by visualizing them in a pink light. This light protects you from their negative thoughts, helps them, and keeps your vibration high—so you can manifest your own wishes.

DID YOU SET A TIME LIMIT?

If your wish hasn't been granted and you asked your angels to help you within a set time limit, you need to know that in the angelic realms, there is no time—so your angels won't necessarily understand your deadlines. Make your angel request again, and this time say, for instance, "Please help me board a train as soon as you're able/help me as soon as possible," rather than "Can I please get to the city in this taxi in the next 15 minutes."

Angels love to help, but they get lots of requests, so make your need obvious and direct but without specific timing. Imagine the wish granted; you don't need desperation in order to be heard.

IS EGO INVOLVED?

Ask honestly if any ego is involved in your wish. Deepak Chopra says: "The ego is our self-image, not our true self." When you ask your angels for help, ask from the place of your soul, from what you feel, rather than what you think you should have. Asking without ego is asking from the place of your true self, without judging yourself or others.

IS IT YOUR DESTINY?

The final reason why your wish may not be granted is that what you are asking for is not right for you. Angels intervene to help you stay on your life path, which means that you, as a soul, are destined to have certain experiences, good and bad. Angels cannot protect you from your soul-destined experiences, but they can support you through them. For example, angels may not be able to prevent the death of a beloved relative, but you can request that they help you accept support from others through the pain of bereavement—which they will always do. You only have to ask.

TRUST, TRUST, TRUST

Don't think about your wish after you've made it. Trust your angels to get to work.

44 Five Special Angel Prayers

Chamuel, for Love and Courage

Archangel Chamuel can help bring you courage, giving you the love and strength to keep going when all else seems to have failed. At these times, you might just have yourself to rely upon, and no one else around to support you. Chamuel sees the bigger picture—his name means "He who sees God." He is a bringer of harmony in relationships, and can help you give and receive more love. When you accept your angel's unconditional love for you and all other beings, you live from the heart and have more love to share. Love is multiplied.

CHAMUEL'S PRAYER

Below is Chamuel's prayer. When you feel no one is beside you, Chamuel will be there. Call upon him for help by saying:

> *Chamuel, help me now and come near.*
> *Lend me courage, be my strength,*
> *Help me accept the gift of love.*
> *Hear my prayer.*
> *Thank you.*

Say this to yourself quietly or out loud, saying "Thank you" when you are ready. This prayer sounds very simple, but the act of acknowledging that you are ready to receive help opens your heart to love.

LEARNING TO RECEIVE

This ritual helps you generate self-compassion and courage. So often we are much harder on ourselves than we would ever be on our closest friends. Day to day, we are beset by a million tasks to do, then berate ourselves for not doing them. There are always people to help us, but when you are stressed or in conflict, it's hard to see them. Yet these helpers are your angels' messengers.

When you feel overwhelmed, rest for just a moment and open up your palms. See light pouring into each palm. Meditate on this, on the receiving, and ask your angels to help you. To receive, you need to be able to feel humility. Sometimes it is easier to be giving to others, because conversely this can feel more empowering, that you are at least busy and doing something, but this just means that you avoid dealing with your own problems. Take a leap of faith. Breathe. Be ready to receive.

Say Chamuel's prayer three times.

Now step back and become a witness—observe what shows up in the next day or two that's positive, rather than continue the struggle to overcome every problem you face on your own. You might feel a tingling down one side of your body when your angels or Chamuel are near. When this happens, know that your prayer is being answered. Your angels will never leave you to fight alone, just invite them to join you. You can say Chamuel's prayer whenever you need to; there is no limit to his help.

You might like to place a pink angel for Chamuel on your altar for seven days after practicing the ritual, because this symbolizes the time of creation—when you create a happier future, with more space for love and compassion for yourself and the new helpers coming into your life.

Michael, to Help You Let Go

Archangel Michael is the angel of truth, protection, and decisions. His name means "He who is as God." He helps you cut the ties that bind you. These ties are metaphors for relationships and other issues that are holding you back. Some ties are subtle, others have a more obvious grip, and they are held in place by your emotional investment in the situation. It is worth contemplating whether your ties are happy or simply habit, and what you may need to let go of to move forward.

Archangel Michael is often shown with a sword and a shield. His sword helps you cut the ties that bind, and banish fear, and his shield means that he will protect you as you go through the transition. Cutting the ties can involve a period of bereavement, a transition phase that might feel uncomfortable. Be gentle with yourself during this time, knowing that you are protected by Michael as you move forward in life.

WHEN IT'S TIME TO LET GO OF THE PAST

* Sit comfortably and close your eyes. Ground, protect, and open up to your angels (see pages 9–10), following the rhythmic sound of your breath. Call in your guardian angel to be with you throughout the ritual. Really feel the presence of your guardian angel with all your senses—color, touch, smell, inner vision, intuition, sound.

When you are ready, call upon Archangel Michael, saying his prayer three times.

Feel an image forming of the person or issue you need to leave behind. Let the image become stronger as you breathe. What do you feel? Do you see the connection between you and the person or issue? You might feel the emotions behind your relationship as different colors, or as physical cords, or chains, or even sticky threads like a spider's web. Let your senses summon all the feelings you have for this person or situation.

MICHAEL'S PRAYER

Whenever you need the strength to let go, call upon Michael by saying his prayer three times:

Michael, help me now and come near.
Protect me, show me truth, give me insight,
Let the past go so I can move on.
Hear my prayer.
Thank you.

Now see whatever image you have shrink to a miniature, as if you were stepping back from a large photograph and shrinking it to the size of a thumbnail. See Archangel Michael take up his sword and cut the bond between you and this now tiny image, which fades and dissolves into light.

Stay with this process as long as you need to, then return your focus to your breathing for a few minutes. When you are ready, thank your guardian angel and Archangel Michael, open your eyes, and close down (see page 11).

LETTING GO OF ADDICTION

You can also use Michael's prayer and his meditation to let go of negative attitudes toward yourself. If you suffer from low self-esteem or repetitive negative thoughts, or are struggling with addiction, such as smoking or unhealthy eating, for example, modify the prayer to "Let go of my xx" and state your problem. Michael will help. Do consult your doctor or other healthcare provider for advice if you need to. You might like to ask Michael to help you write down or mentally review what you need to say before an appointment, too, as he supports true communication.

Raphael, for Healing

Raphael means "God has healed," and so he is the angel of healing. He is also associated with joy, peace, and knowledge. These can be seen perhaps as the outcome of healing and recovery; the experience of illness often makes us wiser, and brings relief, happiness, and peace of mind. Raphael is usually linked with green, the color of healing and of the heart chakra.

RAPHAEL'S PRAYER

Raphael, help me now and come near.
Bring me healing.
May you bring healing to me [or name others]
And peace to us all.
Hear my prayer.
Thank you.

BE THE HEALER

We are all healers. We all have the ability to soothe and comfort others and change our world for the better with our words, thoughts, intentions, and actions. You can have a profound healing effect on everyone in your life. This prayer is a call to Raphael, the angelic doctor, to help ourselves and/or others, but it also awakens the healer within.

Angelic healing means allowing your angels to channel their healing light through you to a person or pet, so that they may begin to heal themselves wherever possible. In essence, we do not heal—but our angels do. We just need to allow this process to happen by becoming a pure channel for our angels.

Healing with angels is safe. You cannot cause harm by gently laying one or both hands on people or your pets (provided you are not touching an area that is sore or infected). However, do not try this if you have drunk alcohol the same day (even just a little), as this can disrupt the flow of healing energy.

Hands-on Healing: Humans and Animals

Before you begin, wash your hands. Make sure the person or animal you are working with is in a comfortable position, and that you can sit comfortably, too.

* Follow the grounding and protection ritual and call in your guardian angel, who will help you connect with Archangel Raphael (see page 13). See a column of light flowing from the crown of your head through to Raphael, then allow his healing energy to pass back down through your crown, third eye, throat, and heart chakras (see page 12) then down both arms and into the palms of your hands. Say Raphael's prayer either aloud or to yourself three times.

* Now rub your palms together and gently place one or both hands on the person or animal. Feel the energy circuit connect, as a flow of green light pouring into their body.

* The next part is tricky: don't do anything. Be empty. Witness your unwanted thoughts floating by and disappearing up into a blue sky. With your mind quiet, use your senses to attune to Raphael (noticing sound, touch, color in your mind's eye). Really feel his energy moving through your body (this is why you need to feel empty, so that you can be filled with his energy). At this point your palms may begin to feel hot. This is normal.

* You might stay in this position for a few moments, or feel guided to move elsewhere on the body. Always check that the person is comfortable for you to touch them there. If you are with an animal, sense their response if and when you move your hands. You can also check with Raphael or your guardian angel if you're unsure about moving position, but you will find that your body often knows what to do.

* You might continue the healing for a few moments or longer. You will know when it's time to remove your hand because the energy will shift and the connection will feel lighter. You may feel as if you were being told to step back. If so, gently remove your hand(s) and step away. Shake your hands and touch the floor. This sends

any excess energy back to Mother Earth and grounds the healing. Thank your guardian angel for sharing the healing experience, and close down (see page 11).

You might also like to try the self-healing and distant healing techniques in Tip 12.

Uriel, for Seeing the Light

Archangel Uriel is the bringer of light. He is known as the Angel of Presence, and his name means "God is my light," or "God is my fire." He stands for creativity, inventiveness, problem-solving, and revealing your life path. He is the

flash of inspiration that shows the way ahead, the light of spirit that illuminates the truth. His element is Earth, and he has long been associated with thunder and earthquakes. As thunder is the sound of lightning, his gift is the flash of knowing, the thunderbolt of realization.

Uriel is often depicted holding a book, symbolizing his knowledge, and standing before a radiant sun. He offers joy and sunshine. It has been said as far back as the thirteenth century that saying the name of Uriel ten times in the morning brings good fortune for the day ahead.

URIEL'S PRAYER

Uriel, help me now and come near.
Bring me the light of knowledge.
Show me my path, make it clear.
Hear my prayer.
Thank you.

ILLUMINATE YOUR LIFE PATH

Find a pen and notepad, and go to a quiet place. Light a candle for Uriel, to honor him with fire energy. Ground and protect yourself, then call in your guardian angel (see pages 9–10). If you have a question, write it down as simply as possible. Be specific; for example, you could say: "Where will my next job be?" or "Should I retrain?" If you already have a career dream, write that down as a wish, such as: "To be a teacher/to travel/to study/to run a new business." Now take out the vowels from your question or wish. For example, "To be a teacher" would become "Tbtchr." Write this down three times, running the words together, on a small, square piece of paper:

Tbtchrtbtchrtbtchr

This is your mantra.

* Fold each corner of the paper into the center, as if you were making an envelope. Say Uriel's prayer three times. Your guardian angel will help you make the connection with Uriel.

* Now take the candle and pour a few drops of hot wax onto the center of the envelope to make a wax seal. Let the wax set, then extinguish the candle flame and place the envelope on your altar. Leave it there for seven days, as seven is one of the numbers of creation.

* Thank your angels, and look for the signs of their guidance over the next week. You may be shown your answer in the page of a magazine you come across, on a billboard, or through the words of a friend, for example. Seeing the signs of an angel in your daily life (see Tip 1)—from a feather to pennies on the street—tells you that you are on your destined path.

Gabriel, for Self-Acceptance and Creativity

Archangel Gabriel is the angel of the Annunciation, who told Mother Mary that she would conceive a son, Jesus. He is the angel of hope, messages, revelations, and guidance (he also helps with conception and children—see Tip 10). His flower is the lily, symbol of purity, and in many paintings of him he is shown with a three-petaled lily, the fleur de lys, which represents the Holy Trinity. Three is a dynamic number. When you see threes, this is a message from God and the universe, delivered by Gabriel, to help you see the potential for change, urging you to accept the gifts you have and get creative with them.

Setting your intention to explore your talents tells the universe that you are willing to believe in yourself and embrace change. Gabriel will hold you as you go through the transformation; it doesn't matter if your wishes are life-changing intentions, such as being a parent, or a small project, such as making a birthday card. Are you wrestling with or searching for inspiration for a writing project? If so, call upon Gabriel, who helps writers and makes the words flow. Angels always fix the source, not the symptom. This often comes down to self-belief and self-acceptance, like tending a garden from which everything else can grow. If you need support in accepting yourself— particularly your psychic gifts—you can wear a

moonstone pendant over your heart or higher heart chakra. Moonstone is one of Gabriel's crystals.

Gabriel can communicate with you in dreams, and help you understand the messages in them. Do you need help finding and following your dreams and goals? Gabriel will empower you to do this. His name means "God is my strength."

GABRIEL'S PRAYER

Gabriel, help me now and come near.
Bring me hope and guide me
So I accept who I am and can be.
Hear my prayer.
Thank you.

GET CREATIVE IN YOUR DREAMS

Before you sleep, prepare your bedroom. You can scent the room with a soothing essential oil such as lavender, which helps promote relaxation. Add a couple of drops to the water bowl of an aromatherapy burner, let it burn for 10–20 minutes, then blow out the candle before you get into bed. Alternatively, spray your bedroom with an angel–dreams mist made with two drops of lavender essential oil and two drops of neroli or clary sage essential oil diluted in about 1 fl. oz. (30ml) of spring water in a mister bottle (dedicate the mist by following the ritual in Tip 27).

* Now ground, protect, and open up (see pages 9–10), making a strong connection with your angels. Write down what you want to do. Write your message as three simple words on a piece of paper or your angel journal, or you can use the notes application on your phone. So, if you are hoping to conceive, you might write your name, your partner's name, and the word "child." If you're working on a project, you could write the following message: "Book/writing/success," expressing the object (book), what you need help with (writing), and how you want to feel (success). Give the note page the title "Gabriel."

* Say Gabriel's prayer three times. Now ask Gabriel and your guardian angel to show you a way forward in your dreams. When you are ready, close down (see page 11).

Look for signs of three the next day. This is confirmation that your angels have heard your prayer, and are working on your wish.

You might also like to read the dream angels tip on page 68.

Keep asking

Angels never run out of wishes for you. Whatever you need, keep asking, and experience the joy of inviting angels into your life.

Thank you, My Angels

part two:

The Angel Directory

44 Angels

ADVACHIEL *(Adnachiel)*

Angel of education, optimism, vision, perspective, and creativity. Ruler of the month of November and the sign of Sagittarius.

AMBRIEL *(Ambiel)*

The parking angel. A problem-solver, he brings versatility, adaptability, and communication. Ruler of the month of May and the sign of Gemini.

AMNITZIEL

The angel of empathy, originality, and intuition. Ruler of the month of February and the sign of Pisces.

ANAEL *see* Haniel

ARARIEL

Arariel presides over water and fish; he is the fishermen's angel, helping them land a good catch.

ARCHANGEL ARIEL

Ariel means "lion of god." He is an archangel of nature, healing, and spiritual development.

ARMISAEL

The angel of the womb. The Talmud says to call upon Armisael to help mother and child during pregnancy.

ARCHANGEL AURIEL

Auriel is an archangel of destiny and the divine feminine, moon magic, and life phases. He is a protector of children.

ARCHANGEL AZRAEL

Angel of bereavement, bringing comfort. He guides departed souls to heaven.

ARCHANGEL BARACHIEL *(Barakiel, Barkiel, Barbiel)*

Chief of the guardian angels. Archangel of imagination, chance, strength, lightning (and intuitive flashes), and psychic development. Ruler of the month of October and the sign of Scorpio.

ASMODEL *(Tual)*

The angel of beauty and self-esteem. Ruler of the month of April and the sign of Taurus.

CAMBIEL

The angel of idealism, novelty, and independence.

CASSIEL

Sheds tears for humanity; offers self-compassion, harmony, serenity, and temperance.

CATHETEL

Angel of gardens and nature.

ARCHANGEL CHAMUEL *(Camael)*

This archangel's name means "He who sees God." Archangel of bravery, courage, and justifiable anger; helps find lost objects.

ETH

An angel of time. Helps things run on schedule.

ARCHANGEL GABRIEL

Means "God is my strength." The archangel of dreams, messages, joy, light, peace, hope, west, guidance, and revelation. Ruler of the month of January and the sign of Aquarius.

HAMALIEL

Hamaliel is the angel of healing, health, and relationships in your workplace. Ruler of the month of August and the sign of Virgo.

ARCHANGEL HANIEL *(Hanael, Anael, Aniel)*

His attributes are love, relationships, growth, healing, communication, and protection. Ruler of the month of December and the sign of Capricorn.

ARCHANGEL ISRAFEL

In Islam, Israfel is one of four archangels, along with Mikhail, Jibrail, and Izra'il.
He is an angel of resurrection and music.

ARCHANGEL JOPHIEL *(Yophiel, Zophiel)*

Jophiel means "Beauty of God." She is the angel of joy, happiness, and vitality. She is a companion of Archangel Metatron.

LAILAH

Angel of conception, who protects our spirit when we are being born.

MACHIDIEL

Meaning "Fullness of God," Machidiel is an angel of assertiveness, impulsiveness, individuality, and self-belief. He is one of the four angels of Malkut, the sephirot on the Tree of Life in Kabbala, which relates to spiritual wisdom. Ruler of the month of March and the sign of Aries.

ARCHANGEL MELCHIZEDECK

Melchizideck, meaning "The god Zedek is my king," may relate to his earthly existence, mentioned in the Bible, as the priest-king of ancient Jerusalem. In ascension work and healing, he is linked with the ascended master Saint Germain, and is associated with Christ-consciousness, spiritual evolution, and justice.

ARCHANGEL METATRON

The archangel of prayer and wisdom. Represents the divine spark of God within us, and is also known as the heavenly scribe. Considered the king of the angels, Metatron had an earthly existence as the prophet Enoch. He is the guardian of guardian angels and the tallest angel in heaven.

ARCHANGEL MICHAEL

Michael's name means "Who is as God." Chief of the archangels, Michael is an angel of peace and the conqueror of Satan. Michael's gifts to us are communication, problem-solving, repentance, sleep, strength, and letting the past go. He takes away negativity and fear, and is an archangel of protection and patience. Michael is also the Angel of Israel.

MIHR

The angel of friendship, light, and love. In Persian lore, Mihr is an angel of judgment and divine mercy.

ARCHANGEL MURIEL

Angel of secrecy, vulnerability, sensitivity, and self-reflection, she protects the creatures of the sea. Ruler of the month of June and the sign of Cancer.

ARCHANGEL ORIEL *see* Auriel

PHANUEL

Angel of hope, peace, and repentance.

PISTIS SOPHIA

Means "faith" and "wisdom." In gnostic beliefs, she is the earthly mother. In ascension work and healing, she is linked with the Ascended Master Lady Kwan Yin.

ARCHANGEL RAGUEL *(Raguil, Rasuil, Rufael)*

Archangel of reconciliation, forgiveness, and new friendships.

ARCHANGEL RAPHAEL

Meaning "God has healed," Raphael is the archangel of healing, hope, joy, peace, knowledge, science, prayer, light, love, and wisdom. A guardian of the tree of life in the Garden of Eden, he is the healer of both mankind and the earth.

ARCHANGEL RAZIEL

Raziel means "Secret of God." He is the cosmic father, an archangel of knowledge and mysteries, and the author of *The Book of the Angel Raziel*, a Kabbala text (see Further Reading, page 144).

ROCHEL

The angel who helps find lost objects.

SACHLUPH

The angel of plants.

SADRIEL

Angel of order and tidiness; call upon him to help traffic flow.

SAMAEL

Archangel of abundance and the harvest.

ARCHANGEL SANDALPHON

An angelic prince, whose name means "brother" or "co-brother." The twin brother of Archangel Metatron. Sandalphon is the archangel of earth healing, absent healing, and prayer. He is believed to have lived on earth as the prophet Elijah.

ARCHANGEL SERAPHIEL

Seraphiel is the ruler of the seraphim, the highest order of angels, who have six wings and sing a hymn of praise to God. In ascension work and healing, Seraphiel is linked with karma clearing and the Ascended Master Seraphis Bey.

Angels of the Days of the Week

Sunday: Michael
Monday: Gabriel
Tuesday: Chamuel
Wednesday: Raphael
Thursday: Sachiel
Friday: Haniel
Saturday: Cassiel

Angels of the Months

January: Cambiel
February: Amnitziel
March: Machidiel
April: Asmodel (Tual)
May: Ambriel
June: Muriel
July: Verchiel
August: Hamaliel
September: Uriel
October: Barachiel
November: Advachiel
December: Haniel

Channeled Messages

These channeled messages are for daily inspiration. You can read them each morning before you begin your day (substitute "me" for "you," or add the name of someone you want to send love and healing to). You can also copy them onto homemade angel cards, and choose one every day or each week as an affirmation.

Your angels love you
Your angels are here to guide and help you
Your angels do not judge
Your angels will always help you fulfill your life's purpose
Your angels lead you away from danger
Your angels' love is unconditional
When angels are near, destiny is at work
Your angels' love helps you be more sensitive and compassionate
Knowing angels means you are never alone in the world
Angels help heal your pain
You can trust your angels
Angels hear you when you talk to them
Angels can give you the courage to walk away
Your angels help you create beauty
Angels love children and always try to protect them
Talking with angels connects you with your true self
When you feel your angels' love, everyone benefits.

TAHARIAL

The angel of the home, and an angel of purity; the domestic-helper angel.

ARCHANGEL TZADKIEL, TSADKIEL *see* Zadkiel

ARCHANGEL TZAPHKIEL *(Tsaphkiel)*

The cosmic mother; angel of femininity, contemplation, and nurturing.

ARCHANGEL URIEL

Uriel means "Fire of God" or "Light of God." The leader of the angels of light, who illuminate truth and help the earth. He can help you find your life path, and is an angel of peace. .

VERCHIEL

An angel of loyalty and courage. Ruler of the month of July and the sign of Leo.

ARCHANGEL ZADKIEL *(Tzadkiel, Tsadkiel, Hesediel)*

Zadkiel means "Righteousness of God." He is the archangel of memory, judgment, justice, mercy, and knowledge; he helps you make changes, improve your career, and keep sight of your goals.

ZURIEL

Zuriel means "My rock is God." He boosts brain-power, banishes ignorance, and protects newborn babies. Ruler of the month of September and the sign of Libra

Index

Acknowledgments

Tom Lumbrazo, for his cloud angel experience: www.whenangelstouch.com; tom@whenangelstouch.com

Geri Sullivan, for "I am an angel" (page 74)

Hayley Newton, the client in the story of Mother Mary (page 118)

Jackie Cox, the Selfridges psychic (page 24)

Hulya Mehmet, for angel coffee-cup readings (page 27)

Daphne Roubini, for her wisdom on friendship (page 124)

Diane Hall, for her "upgrade" experience (page 104)

Sheila Young, for her crystal knowledge

Special thanks to Cindy Richards, Lauren Mulholland, and all the team at CICO; our agent, Chelsey Fox; Sarah Perkins, for her gorgeous illustrations; and, of course, our angels.

Further reading

The Book of the Angel Raziel

The Book of Tobit

The Book of Enoch

A Dictionary of Angels, Gustav Davidson, (New York: Free Press/Simon & Schuster, 1967)